Soul Orientation
The Dance of Reflective Relationship

by Kiera D. Laike, IRW

First published by Dog Ear Publishing
4010 W. 86th Street, Ste H
Indianapolis, IN 46268
www.dogearpublishing.net

ISBN: 978-1-4575-2476-9

This book is printed on acid-free paper.

Printed in the United States of America

This book is dedicated to:

The memory of my reflected relationship star form.

Humans emerged between water and earth, between air and fire — not to have dominion over them, but as the embodied reflection of all that is in the spaces in between. Therefore, there is no higher person or order; there is only reflective relationship.

—Kiera D. Laike, IRW

Table of Contents

Note to the reader:

The practice taught in this book awakens our sensing nature of being. To truly experience human energetic soul-orientated reflected relationship, we must release the need to understand everything cognitively. Cognitive understanding is not a prerequisite for Embodiment. To aid you, I have provided many scientific, personal, and mathematical examples to support your cognitive brain - thus enabling you to use anchors as you make the journey beyond cognition into Embodied sensing.

For those who feel they would benefit from having the practice segment in audio format, all practice segments in this book are available as MP3 voice files for purchase and download (or on CD) at www.SensologyInstitute.com.

Safety Note:

The contents of this book may only be safely taught by a Certified Embodied Practice Teacher. Certified teachers have the ability to hold and create the proper spheres and containers in which the practice must be taught. To clarify this point, I hand-wrote this entire book while I was connected to all that was in me – so that the reading of the words from the pages creates the containers.

—Kiera D. Laike, IRW

Introduction

To truly awaken one must develop the ability to attach to everything - this cannot be accomplished through making everything the same or from a man-made organized philosophy or structure. True awakening emerges from the mechanism to establish and maintain relationship with everything. This ability can only be present through a pulsating process within the container of the Universe. Soul orientation is the journey to establish the mechanism to awaken these pulse containers and enter the dance of reflective relationship.

—Kiera D. Laike, IRW

Soul orientation is the presence of the energetic mechanisms in body, which enable us to be in communication across time and space. Once we establish these connections we are fully awake, each and every moment of the day and night in complete Embodied soul experience.

Soul orientation develops out of the energetic development of humans. Our human development is complete via our sensing nature of being in body. Soul orientation guides us to what our position is in body, how and what we reflect in the Universe. This reflection provides the mechanisms of amazing pure experience.

As humans, we were walled off, which separated us from the inner mechanism of our human DNA'S energetic evolution. This has created an abyss that has gotten bigger during the last 10,000 years of our evolution. In an abyss, we must possess internal guidance systems in order to manage and not lose our way, self, or soul essence.

Today, all of us are born into the human field. The human field is an electromagnetic pulse field which all humans communicate with. Since humans are energetic developmental beings, when born we only communicate with the human field. Currently the human field possesses no information as to how to get out of the abyss and we have no internal guidance system. The human field continues to dictate to us what to create. Without soul orientation, one has no mechanism of knowing if they are creating in or out of the human field. Without this self-made organized system, we are in the position of always searching outside of ourselves for the next self-help book, modality of therapy, religion, or the latest guru. One of my clients described it best. For ten years, she read every self help and new age philosophy book she could get her hands on. Three months into Embodied Practice she had been working on developing the internal guidance systems and relayed her experience of the previous decade's journey:

"Ever searching, I constantly read self-help and spiritual books - with each book, I became more paralyzed and overwhelmed. I knew the information in the books was wrong for others and wrong for me. So, my knowledge of what was wrong with me hurt even deeper and became an even greater bur-

den - until I felt so trapped that I thought I was dying. A breath of air has come, now that I can sense myself and make change inside."

—Kiera's client

Through Embodied Practice, we can learn to know we are in the human field.

Without soul orientation and our developed energetic self, we cannot respond to our energetic nature of being so we can know when we are communicating with our energetic nature of being.

Energetic Nature of Being

To understand who we are as energetic beings we have to go back to the beginning of time and space - to the initial pulse in and the initial pulse out, to our knowing the creation of matter. This pulsing process or continuous pulse in and out is the underlining fabric of the Universe. The pulsating process and its connection to matter and particles is how communication occurs across time and space. We have to go back to when the particles clustered and formed into suns or planets. As these suns and planets formed they developed a mechanism of connection to the cascading pulse process across the fabric of the Universe.

As a human being, our soul body is created by our soul essence. Our energetic development begins before our physical development. Our soul essence is energy living as oriented photon light waiting to create our physical form like the gravity of the sun that formed the planets. When a Universe is created, particles of matter cluster in a group in the fabric of space to organize and form a sun. The sun then creates a container of gravity, which then becomes the container of forming a solar system.

A soul essence is a collection of photon light particles that organizes with the containers of solar systems. Human soul essence forms the soul body in our first container, the womb of the mother. Here we begin our journey of our energetic development. This energetic developmental journey should take 15-21 years to be able establish our energetic connections to the cascading pulse process that cascades across the fabric of space.

Our soul essence is like a blueprint for development of the body and ultimately the soul of that lifetime. Soul and soul essence are not the same thing, yet they need to communicate together to be fully in the pulse process of reflective relationship.

So, like the matter particles forming planets ultimately developing their mechanism of communication with the pulse process in the fabric of space, we as human beings develop our mechanisms of communication with each life.

Once we are born into this world, our soul cannot stay in contact with the information of the soul essence until we develop the energetic mechanisms. We are born into a state of amnesia. We remember bits and pieces; yet, to remember the whole picture, we have to develop fully and gather our soul essence and ultimately each past life footprint.

The soul essence is the least defined or understood. It is hard to grasp a cognitive understanding of something that is everywhere, yet nowhere. Our essence is an organized energy coming in and out of being. In order to come into and out of existence, there must be a mechanism for doing this. For soul essences that choose the human journey, this mechanism is the creation of the human body and the soul footprint from that incarnation called past life footprints. In each life, we create a footprint that is the sum of the soul essence creation and reflection into the body and then the lifetime experience. On death, our bio-photon light leaves our body and is fused into a past life footprint in the human field.

A lot of confusion, conflicting information, what our souls are, control over what happens to the soul, and how the soul is created exists in society. It is my deepest longing that my knowing will release us from confusion.

Our Soul Loses Connection with our Soul Essence

How do we make it through the journey of the abyss, complete our energetic development, and regain our communication with our soul essence? Embodied Practice offers the mechanism of this journey. Soul essence lives within us in the third ventricle, the waterbed in the center of our head which, when developed, has the ability to be in constant communication with the Universe. The soul essence contains the perfect blueprint of our energetic self, yet cannot be constructed without the containers needed to activate the structures in the vortexes.

Think of the soul essence as a seed. Much like when the seed of an oak tree, rose plant, or corn stalk is planted in the ground, the seed already has a code that will help it find its way to grow. If we put the seed in the ground, insisting it not communicate with itself, and instead have it communicate with something outside of itself, then we would never have an oak tree, a rose bloom, or a piece of corn. The seed (soul essence) has to listen to its own self and then express itself. If we lack the containers of soil, water, and sun, then no rose, tree, or corn could grow.

The seed then begins to grow into a tree. The tree is the soul. The tree in physical form is not protected as is the seed. Once the tree grows, the seed for a time is no more, until the tree fully develops and creates new seeds. The tree then experiences exposure to the sun, wind, rainstorms, humans trimming etc.; the tree also becomes the reflection of what happens to it.

In our example, the tree is representative of our body, as it is developed out of the soul essence communication with chromosomes in the seed. When the tree has sprouted, the seed for a time is no more. Until we develop, we can lose communication with soul essence. When the tree emerges, it grows more seeds, which is the soul's way of reconnecting to essence. When we achieve energetic development we are able to gather our soul essence to get us back in communication. This is done firstly through the third ventricle, the physical center of the head.

As our physical body develops, our soul automatically starts searching for our soul essence. Meanwhile, the soul essence never changes (except from severe situations). It is waiting patiently for the soul to start communicating with it so that it can provide the map or essence code. Since the soul essence is in communication with the Universe, once the soul finds the soul essence, it will start to communicate with the energy in the Universe through the soul essence. This safely happens within the embodied practice containers, supported in the first two levels of practice by the Embodied Teacher and through the container of this book.

There are obstacles for the soul on its quest to find the soul essence, especially in today's world. Often we think we can find our purpose without it. Even if we fall into what our planned path is to be, it will not be satisfying unless we connect through our soul essence.

Lost Without Essence

When you are lost, the first thing you must know before finding the way again is where you are. This is called the point of origin. Once we have our point of origin we need information as to how to get to the next place. We receive information by communicating with what we already know or new information we acquire by communicating outside of ourselves. However, once we go outside of ourselves we are vulnerable to false information. We have to learn how to sift through information that would cause us to become even more lost. Power comes from knowing where we are so we know which way to head.

Point of Orientation is the Beginning of Understanding What Is

If we are holding an egg and we don't know if it is a turtle egg or a bird egg, everything we assign to it or what we do with it could be disastrous; if we put the turtle egg in a bird nest it would die when it hatched. If we buried the bird egg in the sand it would die when it hatched.

Many are in a state of soul death because they cannot connect to their point of orientation or soul essence. It has been lost in a splitting of concepts that humans are psychological beings, biological beings, or a soul. This continues to cascade causing the egg to get buried in the wrong place. Of course, at first when the bird egg was buried in the sand it received heat and support to hatch. Yet it eventually meets its death. In other words, it cannot go on to live life as a bird when not in its right place of orientation.

In soul orientation, we offer an old knowledge that was taken from humanity when the human field was formed – this knowledge is the concept that we are energetic beings, who have formed to have an experience through our human bioelectric body. This vibrational bioelectric experience, miraculous and complicated, gives rise to the first Embodied Principle which gives us a container to begin to follow the ever flowing connections, to pulse process across the Universe. This Embodied Principle is named "The 4x4 To Infinity".

When we can begin to see the Universe as a cascade of energetic interactions through a pulse relationship of expanding and contracting, as outlined in the Baum-Frampton theory (not a big bang, but a "big rift", over and over, the Universes continually expanding and contracting), then we know that to be a part of this pulse relationship we can only be energetic beings.

The longing for awakening has cascaded across the human experience as it has been remembered and recorded. Throughout history, as cultures continued to evolve and new information came to them, as we see and understand it in embodied knowing, a separation occurred and connection was lost. In this loss of connection we fell asleep in some way. The sleep state has given rise to many man-made structures, organizations, philosophies, and religions - all of which reveal the way back to connection, through a God image or source.

In my awakening, this is backwards. The mechanism of connection within the body, because we are developmental beings, must be reestablished before we can once again communicate with the Universe, god, or source. Without any mechanism to communicate with someone, how would we ever know with what or whom we should communicate?

For example, there is a mechanism in the hypothalamic-pituitary-axis which responds to light. When the light leaves (while the sun is setting), hormones are released to promote sleep. The same releasing of hormones occurs when the sun rises. We can (and billions do every day) fall asleep and awake out of synchronization with the rising and setting of the sun. However, when we are out of synchronization, we are not as awake as we could be physically (from a neuropeptide perspective) and our physical health does not attain peak levels that day. The trigger that awakens us, in our example, is the sun - which awakens our mechanism of connection that releases the neuropeptides in the brain. It is the first step to awakening, not fixing or coming up with systems that help us function and connect without awakening to the rising sun. Please don't get hooked on the example, because most of us currently don't have the lifestyle that allows us to rise with sun – we use some structure or aid to support us in awakening. Apply this concept to the connection and communication with the Universe, god, or source. The mechanism must be present for connection, the functioning hypothalamic-pituitary-axis, meeting the rising and setting sun, and it must also be in communication with the sun to fully awaken us. In other words if the mechanism in hypothalamus pituitary axis is faulty, the setting sun will not trigger sleep. The mechanism in the hypothalamus pituitary axis must first be developed, so it can respond to the rising sun. Without this order of mechanism we are not fully awake.

Our example illustrates a structural standpoint, as we understand it in embodied practice. We connect to the equivalent of the rising sun. In other words, we align with the ability of the hypothalamus pituitary axis to connect for awakening (in our body, this is our soul essence) and experience what occurs as we rise with the rising sun. The soul essence is the mechanism of connection. Connection must have a position, its own container, and be in its position on earth, the solar system, and ultimately the Universe. Human evolution through the human field has pulled us so far from these connections that we no longer possess the mechanisms to respond.

Chapter 1

Embodied Practice

Phases of Embodied Practice

For us to emerge and bridge the gap of the past 10,000 years, to connect to our sensing, which guides the evolution of our DNA, a healing practice needed to be brought into form. This awakening led me to develop the three phases of Embodied Practice. Soul orientation, dancing in reflective relationship, emerges slowly through the Healing Practice phase and begins to come in fully in the Pulse Practice phase, and ultimately over lifetimes to Emergence Practice.

Healing Embodied Focused Practice

This is a beautiful practice, where our energetic healing occurs within an embodied sphere. This embodied sphere is created and forged in the electromagnetic field of earth by the Embodied Practice teacher. It is a wonderful womb, providing an energetic protection and containment while one learns the Healing Practice. Embodied containers are in reflective relationship, so while protecting one, they are also being met. In this meeting, one's soul in this lifetime is prepared to gather its own soul essence, ultimately across all incarnations.

During the Healing Practice, the embodied container is critical - for without the container (as the soul gathers its essence), the soul is completely vulnerable to an array of energies that benefit from us not gathering our essence. The energies that benefit (primarily from us not gathering our soul essence or knowing that we are sensing beings) prefer that we do not heal, gather our essence, or remember our sensing nature.

The first level Healing Practice is offered in the following pages of this book, forged in the electromagnetic fields being a container. First, we awaken the third ventricle to begin to house and gather soul essence. Then, we heal our basic energy channels in the body – that gave us our first position between earth and sky, we strengthen our container through the Breath of Life, and lastly we awaken to our sensing vortexes, how they mirror earth, their form and their functions.

Energetic Beings

The Healing Practice slowly awakens in us that all that is created begins in the unseen energy and cascades through human evolution over thousands and hundreds of years. Our energetic ability to communicate determines this evolution and ultimately functional oneness.

Functional Oneness

To understand functional oneness, we will explore the system of communication on a body level. Each of us may have fallen victim to a horrible cold that sweeps through the country in winter. Let us say this cold is both viral and bacterial in nature and invades the body. When this happens, our immune system kicks in and sends out little identifiers (such as NF kappa B) to identify what is causing the problem. Once our immune system identifies it, it asks the body to respond by developing antibodies. In our example, the immune system has been looking for the bacteria or the virus causing the problems. When the system communicates correctly, it identifies the bacteria or virus and we get better.

This is a functional system of communication through our immune system where the communication is on different levels with our spleen, appendix, etc. - all of which produce different kinds of immune responses. The system is talking and therefore it works. Maybe we take vitamin C to support the system or get extra rest - then the system would be able to talk a little faster and we could heal faster.

What would happen if we got that cold or virus and the immune system could not talk or was not able to identify the virus? Maybe it identified a body system, an organ, or some tissue in the body as the problem. In the medical profession, this is called an autoimmune disease; the immune system is not communicating correctly and is falsely identifying normal parts as problems within the body. A common example of this is Hashimoto's disease which occurs when the immune system has misidentified thyroid tissue as a foreign object in the body. When it misidentifies the thyroid tissue and develops antibodies to the thyroid tissue it believes is a foreign object. Then we do not get better and become very sick.

This is a simple understanding of how all the aspects of the immune system work together to help us to get better, but only when the system is communicating and doing what it is supposed to be doing. When our immune system cannot communicate correctly and responds in error, wrongly, then we become ill. The concept of how one immune system could communicate for health and healing and another could communicate to cause ill health is also true in the energetic realm.

Now let's return to the premise that on an energetic level it is our ability to develop and establish communication with and through the soul essence. This energetic communication with our soul essence establishes the functional oneness and energetic evolution of humans. It is a communication system which can perform correctly.

Communication - So What?

Let us say that we travel somewhere alone. We go to a part of the world where we do not know anything about the people, what they eat, or their daily customs. We do not speak a word of their verbal language and they do not speak a word of our verbal language. We are trying to communicate on our own to get something to eat, to know where to stay or what kind of barter or monetary exchange to use.

If we think of this travel example in terms of an energetic language we begin to get a glimpse of our current situation. In the energetic realm we are speaking a language, a language we have forgotten. Over thousands and thousands of years of our evolution, most of us have lost our abilities to listen, respond, sense, and speak the energetic language of the pulse fields of the Universe. Just like traveling to an unknown part of the world, communicating in the energetic realm is difficult at first.

In healing practice, our energetic systems that we use to learn the energetic language are activated. This is just like teaching our immune system to communicate how it is supposed to, instead of misidentifying and causing harm, as in the example of Hashimoto's disease.

When we initiate our healing Embodied Practice, our systems learn. Our energetic language systems are infinitely more complete and complicated than the language of our immune systems. The outcome of learning the energetic language is a more wondrous outcome than how good we feel when our immune system communicates correctly.

Outcome of Purpose

Our lost ability to communicate energetically has placed us at a disadvantage to understand how to get our needs met, or even what our function is. When I look around, listen to people, and see what people are attracted to on the internet, it is usually somebody promising a purpose, a cause, or something that would give somebody a purpose. This is very common since when we are out of communication we do not feel a purpose. It can be like we are in a room full of people but no one is talking to us, we do not really feel like we have a purpose or place being there. Yet when people do talk to us, we feel part of something, fulfilled and feel purposeful. In the same way energetically, because we lost our ability to communicate, we are very focused on identifying our purpose - because energetically we are the person in that room, we are not talking to anyone, and no one is talking to us.

As we begin to heal in Embodied Practice, the quest for purpose just melts away because we come into communication. We are that person at the party everyone is talking to, and the question of purpose does not even come up, because we are in communication, so we are fulfilling our purpose. What we are here to do, in body, is to communicate with all different kinds of things in different ways and have a soul experience in body or matter form.

We live in an era during which autoimmune disease is increasing at such a fast rate that the medical profession can barely get a handle on it. The pharmaceutical profession cannot make new drugs fast enough to keep up with the ever cascading symptoms and problems that come from a wide variety of symptoms that originate from autoimmune disease. Bringing our energetic systems back into correct communication provides the container for our immune system to return to its communication, and ultimately everything else.

Embodied Principle of 4x4 to Infinity (Emergence)

In the opening I dipped our big toe in the concept of the first Embodied Principle 4x4 to Infinity and our need for it to aid us in understanding our experience through the body. So let's stick our foot in and begin to awaken to the Principle of 4x4 to Infinity.

The Embodied Principle of 4x4 to Infinity begins with pulse since all aspects of creation begin with pulse. Our wondrous example of this here on earth is the pulse of the tide, the point of origin of container for emergence of humans. The forming of our moon created the tides and the movement of water supported bacteria population. Tide is the first pulse on earth that birthed into the container. Next, bacteria gave oxygen which created the atmosphere held within the electromagnetic field of earth.

Emergence has infinite points of origin and they all begin in an unseen way just like the creation of the Universe. There are still questions regarding what happened as that energy contracted in and then expanded out, contracting in again and expanding out again to forge the universe. There are four beginning points of orientation which always start the 4x4 to Infinity – those four points of origin are pulse, crystal structure, journey and reflection.

Pulse

Pulse is our first point of origin and we always have this. There is always something that contracts in, some occurrence that causes a contraction in and then a contraction out. Either we would call it a response or just simply the natural thing to occur like a heartbeat. Cell membranes do this also. They are incredibly complex and are also containers. All containers have pulse. This is why whenever we talk about emergence we begin with pulse, because it is pulse that creates containers. Containers then dictate the next step of creation.

Don't worry if reading this makes your brain hurt. Just stay with your breath and stay with the pause of your breath. The ability to stay with the Pause of the Breath is outlined in the Supplemental Section of the book, under "Settling Breath". Allow the words to come up to you like a wave and recede from you like a wave. Then understanding you will end up immersed in emergence.

Crystal Structure

Crystal structures or some form of them always follow pulse. This is represented in the cell membrane with how the cell receptors receive signals and the resulting protein function response. This response creates the cells ability to morph the cell membrane shape through the activation of the proteins to accept things, like insulin, or not accept things. This then tells the body, through sending signals to the inside of the cell, information about what to do, what's happening, and dictates a cellular response.

The structures in the cell membrane, from an energetic standpoint, fit our definition of crystals.

They change shape, grow, and are a mechanism of communication. This is the role of the crystal structure.

Stay with your Pause of the Breath as you read. Let the words wash over you like waves.

In 2005, Masaru Emoto's book, *The Hidden Messages in Water,* brought to light that water holds information. Mr. Emoto froze samples of water that had been exposed to different words, music, and emotions - then he looked at the frozen samples under a microscope. He found that water exposed to influences that would be considered loving, kind, and altruistic materialized perfectly formed crystals. Those influenced by negativity were malformed. The fractal patterns were not clear and there was distinction. The water had held onto the information that was presented to it, displaying it in the crystal structures of the water.

Journey

Crystal structures always initiate a process of one type, resulting in an initiation of a journey. This is the cell membrane's response to what is happening. A cell's journey is always initiated by something.

As an example, when cortisol gets called in the body it signals insulin to enter cell membranes. As cortisol increases the cell membranes' ability to read insulin, take in insulin, deal with insulin, or all of the above, diminishes or down regulates. This then creates a difficult situation for the body and sends it on a journey. Of course, if high cortisol is a chronic condition, it would get stuck in the journey and one begins insulin resistance. One would not come out of the journey and would remain insulin resistant. In other words, cortisol levels that are consistently too high create insulin resistance. The cell stops trying to deal with the situation with insulin and simply responds to it marginally.

What is present in the information of crystal structures creates the journey. In our example, it is a negative one, yet when we learn to control our cortisol production, a journey of normal insulin signaling can begin. Just as our soul self-entry dictates how we will be in communication with life, crystal structures dictate our journey in life.

Reflections

Our next aspect is reflection. What happens in the journey of the cell membrane is reflected in all of the body. Continuing with the example of insulin resistance, the insulin resistance causes all kinds of metabolic problems in the body. It down regulates dopamine and causes depression. It changes testosterone and estrogen in the body, and usually causes abdominal obesity or excess fat. This is reflected in the rest of the body. However, if we used the previous example of the cell receptor, which would continue to respond and handle the insulin, it would also reflect throughout the rest of the body. The reflection would be the opposite; no depression, a healthier body, and no metabolic syndrome.

4x4 to Infinity Embodied Principle of 4x4 to Infinity Aspects

Pulse, crystal structure, journey, and reflection all have an aspect. An aspect is an action. The four points of origin and their corresponding aspects are: form, flow, function, and relationship. These aspects each have their unique pulse relationship with each other.

Form

Once a pulse occurs, form follows. The universe pulsed inward and formed matter. For instance, a sun forms beginning with pulse and then the planets form around it. Pulse always brings something into form.

Flow

Once earth is formed, she takes on her orbit (flow). Her mantle flows - the trade winds, the tides, all aspects of flow that come from form.

Function

Each flow has a function. Each part flowing has a function. The orbit keeps our earth planet with biological life and the trade winds balance heat within the planet.

Relationship

Relationship is how the energy particles, photon light, structures etc., exchange or share energy or matter. The sun's solar energy is exchanged with earth in complex patterns through the four layers of earth's atmosphere.

Embodied Principle of 4x4 to Infinity

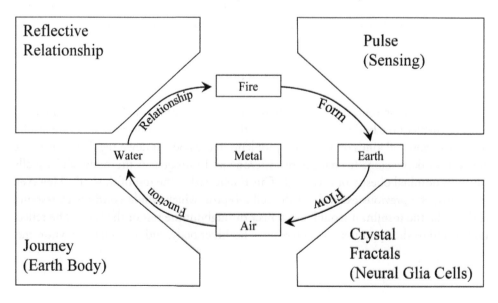

Chapter 2

Soul Orientation

*That which tells us how to develop and what is created, when not in com-
munication with everything we do not know, will develop and create that
which should never be brought into being. Without our soul orientation we
find ourselves experiencing the latter.*

- Kiera D. Laike IRW

Communication: The Beginning

Life is experience occurring through a sequence beyond words through mechanisms of communication on more levels than we think we can keep up with. For example, at any given
moment in time we are receiving 5000 signals, yet only possess the cognitive ability to process
300 of the signals received. The ability to have what one needs to process and interpret the
other 4,700 signals comes from the complex energetic development of our human energy system.

This energetic process to sense information and line up accordingly is seen in how the chromosomes line up and the ability of DNA snips to turn on and off. Since we as humans have
lost our mechanism as energetic sensing beings, it would follow that our chromosomes would
not line up and the DNA would lose its ability to turn on and off correctly. Many experts in
autism treat it by working with DNA snips that are turned off but should be on.

In the sea of light signaling all occurring in the unseen realm, the Embodied Principles
are our containers of creating our energetic development once again.

Our First Embodied Principle: The Principle of Orientation

The Principle of Orientation was birthed out of the knowledge that we occupy no particular place in space. Thus, in order to know where we are, to orient ourselves, we must
be able to project three intersecting lines, each line formed by two places in time and
space, so we can know and see where we are, and begin our communication with all.

Let's back up. Copernicus and mathematics awaken us to this within the realm of science.

Copernicus was the first man to see that Earth does not occupy the center of the Universe, but
that the sun is in the center of the planetary system. This is the heliocentric system. Before his
discovery, civilization believed the Earth to be the center of the Universe. The Copernicus
Principle shows that Earth did not occupy any particular position in space, as it revolves and
moves through space. This *seeing of what is* gave us the foundation for all of the discoveries
regarding the Universe and solar system since then. Copernicus's Principle demonstrates (in
an amazing way to the modern world) that orientation to "what is" changes what we do – and

it is one of the mechanisms of emergence into awakening to *what is* and to functional one-ness. Just as Copernicus identified the sun as the center point of origin for our planetary system, our soul essence is the point of origin for each of us. If we cannot orientate with our point of origin, our soul essence, we are not going to awaken to the true *what is*. Once we awaken to *what is*, our perception of ourselves and what's around us transforms.

For the space program, a celestial sphere coordinate system was developed to calculate flight paths to the moon. A system utilizing three intersecting lines, each at the end of a fixed place in space was used to navigate the space ship to the moon. In Healing and Focused Embodied Practice, we use the same simple mathematic example of three inter-secting lines to allow us to orient or locate ourselves in body and in space. We begin with three intersecting lines that reside in all of us, which are the backbones of our soul ori-entation. To establish an Embodied Orientation, we use six points that connect with three lines, which intersect at our orientation point. These points and lines that reside in us are a compass to awaken to *what is*.

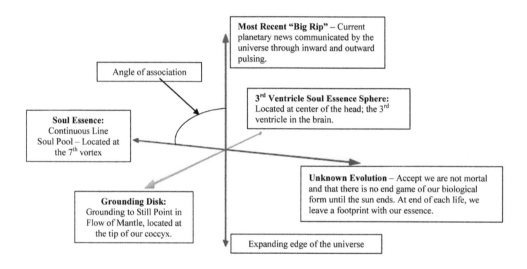

Three Spheres of Orientation

The three intersecting lines can be connected into three spheres of the three aspects of Embodiment.

How We Develop

Through deep communication of my soul essence over the last 25 years of my life, I have brought from remembrance the 13 Energetic Developmental Stages of Humans, housed in my Theory of Sensology, which provide the container for our unique soul essence to express itself through our energetic vortexes. Without the right container or 'energetic developed body,' our soul essence does not reestablish its communication. If the seed is not planted in soil, it will not grow.

At the beginning of each life, the soul essence establishes communication through the vortex that is created when the sperm breaks the outside edge of the egg. Two vortexes become one. In that moment of development, the soul still has connection via its soul essence. It is connected through the fibers of cosmic or space because the body is not yet fully formed. The soul does not communicate or know through the body, it is still in communication through the fibrous strands of the Universe and in communication with its soul essence.

The embryo and soul begin development through direct communication with soul essence and with the fibrous strands of the Universe. This happens in stages. The first stage happens at four to five weeks in the uterus. The heart, which is no bigger than the size of a fingernail, houses valves that are not developed but circulate blood. At this moment in development, the heart is more like a pump and not a container controlling the pulsing of the heart in and out since there are not four chambers to contain. The little developing heart houses the soul, the reflection of the soul essence not the soul essence itself, and communication begins to wane.

When this flow pulse in the embryo occurs, it is as though a veil comes over the soul developing in the body. Instead of having clear 100% communication as it did before it entered the body in essence form, the soul now communicates through this veil around this pulse field or flow fields of the body - journeying to develop an energetic body to reestablish communication with soul essence and the cascading pulse fields, which the essence is in communication with.

Around seven weeks of gestation, the four chambers of the heart develop. This further magnifies the field and the soul is contained in a stronger and stronger veil.

At nine weeks, all communication to fibrous strands of Universe and soul essence end. At nine weeks until three months, the soul begins the first abyss labyrinth journey into the body. It is waiting, only communicating with the soul essence reflection, without communication to soul essence. There is no communication through the fibrous structure because, although the electromagnetic field of the heart exists, none of the structures or mechanisms in the body has developed yet. Our fibrous structures, with which we will begin our first communication, are not fully developed enough throughout the body. This is very significant because of how the soul handles this time and what happens from three months until a month after birth determines the extent to which the soul makes or completes the first energetic developmental stage called Journey into Form: Soul Self

Entry. This stage creates our first container to begin our energetic journey to bring our soul essence into communication through body soul form.

At three months, the little baby body in the uterus has developed back fascia. This is over the trapezius muscle, which goes across the back of the shoulders and V's down. The fascia tissue comes to a point and enters into the back between the 3rd and 4th Vortex.

All of us have experienced pain, some of us great pain, in that particular part of our body. There is always a significant energetic reason for that and it usually has to do with our fascia or our fibrous strands in our fascia's ability to communicate with information. The least complicated way to understand this is to refer back to how the baby communicates: that the soul communicates through the baby's body with what is in the outside world. In the uterus, the first thing we communicate with is the energy of our mother, literally the energy of her womb. The energy of the womb and what occurs sets our ability to sense. During this time, we deepen our sensing or energetic development by communication with fascia strands. Our fascia strands are the first physical structure to establish communication with unseen energy.

Outcomes of Communication

In the below examples we begin to get an understanding of how our fascia communicates and gives us our experience of life which further determines our continued energetic development.

Example 1: Everything goes well between three months and one month after birth. The baby is born able to communicate with the unseen energy through the strands of its fascia, depicted by the open bare hand ready to meet the world. It processes the unseen energy of the world in full communication through the open pulsating fascia.

Example 2: The pregnancy and birth are so-so. Maybe there is a little bit of difficulty, maybe the mom was not exactly happy about her pregnancy, maybe her own vortexes are not very developed. Her energy centers are underdeveloped and the soul of the baby is trying to communicate through the fibrous strands and is not getting many signals back because the mother's vortexes are sending few. The baby's ability to communicate through the strands of its fascia will meet and experience the world like it is wearing a glove and experiences communication through the glove. Sensing is hampered at all levels in orientation, knowledge of origin, communication with self, and communication with others.

Example 3: There is a lot of difficulty and a lot of confusion during the pregnancy. Maybe there were medical issues with the mother, maybe there was tremendous stress or tragedy during pregnancy, or something significant happened in the birth process. Here, the baby's fibrous strands are born communicating and processing the unseen energy as though through a baseball mitt (heavy leather and padding). Life experience is hampered and often confusing.

Example 4: Nothing goes well or according to expectations for the soul developing within the body. The baby's sensing is the equivalent of a hand with a boxer's glove (heavy thick padding) on it. To try to communicate and process the unseen energy of life through such a thick obstacle creates bonding issues in the baby and significant problems with reality testing.

We have these four examples of the soul experiencing life which creates one of the containers of soul orientation. First, we have a soul experiencing life as a bare hand. The second soul experiences life as though through a hand wearing a glove. The third soul experiences life as though through a baseball mitt, and the fourth soul experiences life through the thick padding of a boxing glove.

Now let us relate these examples to how we sense information in life such as thoughts, emotions, people and situations. Let's say the first bit of information we communicate with is represented by a pine needle. We place the pine needle in the hand of the first soul that is in soul communication. The hand would feel the pine needle, experience the fibrous structure of the pine needle, might get pricked by the pine needle, and may have a spontaneous thought of something that could be done with the pine needle. The hand is in communication with the pine needle, meeting it and being met by it, processing the unseen energy.

In our second example, we place the pine needle into the gloved hand. Unless the glove is thermal for a wilderness trip, people wearing most gloves would be able to know that they have something in their hand. They may not be able feel the fibrous structure and they are probably not going to get pricked by the pine needle. They will not have a deep physiological experience of the pine needle. They may or may not feel met or be able to meet the pine needle depending on a host of other factors.

In our third example, the baseball gloved hand will not really know that they have anything in their baseball glove. There is no meeting or being met. Bonding is disrupted in a significant way.

In our fourth example, the soul born is energetically experiencing the world through the boxing glove – and will feel nothing. Additionally, the soul will experience the weight and binding of the gloves on its fibrous stands in the body, and will most likely misinterpret the pine needle in the glove. This eventually manifests into difficulty with reality testing and bonding.

What does this have to do with soul orientation and how we develop? The soul's journey dictates the containers that the soul creates. This developmental experience in and through the body creates energetic structures that allows the soul essence to come into communication.

Imagine that we are the soul with the boxing gloves on and we have no idea what is in our hand and no ability to interpret anything about it. We would have to rely on other people for details. Someone else might come along, perhaps a teacher or some other person who has declared themselves knowledgeable, or a prescribed religious person, or a new age teacher. The person who has not had soul entry is experiencing life through the boxing glove. The teacher is then projecting their own information about the pine needle. The soul has no sensing of its own. The pine needle represents life information about their soul in the body. We have not begun soul self-entry, so we cannot begin our energetic soul development. We do not even know that we have anything in our hand and we are 100% vulnerable to whatever that other person tells us about the pine needle. We are only in communication with the other. The other person can tell us it's a matchstick, or a piece of hair, or pretty much anything. Because we do not have any experience of what the pine needle is, we cannot communicate through our fibers, like the soul who had soul self-entry, with the pine needle in a bare hand, in communication through the fibers of the hand directly, with what is. The boxing gloved hands have none of this. So we are ever pulled out to get information from someone else, ever separate from our soul in body until we can heal and build the missing containers.

There are a lot of different people in a lot of different places on this spectrum. The person with the glove on would get some information about the pine needle. But they too might look out a little bit, and ask, "Do you have anything in your hand? What are you feeling? What's happening with you?" This is where the person that wears the glove becomes vulnerable to someone else's perception of what is and therefore misses essence communication.

When these things happen to us and we have no way of reestablishing our communication with soul essence, we are very vulnerable to what I call lost in someone else's story, in that state. We have some sense of what's going on for us but we don't have our full story because we don't have our full soul self entry and have not established communication with our soul essence. In addition, we do not have guidance to develop and heal our energetic systems so we can learn the language of the pulse fields of the Universe once again.

If we use the example of a rock instead of a pine needle, this represents a different life experience than the pine needle. The person experiencing life through the boxing glove will still lack all sensing of the rock in their hand. The person with the baseball glove will probably have a sense of the rock. Because they can have a limited sense of the rock, they will probably come up with a few things of what it is and may drop or throw it. The person with the bare hand is going to have a full experience of the rock and may even have a sense of what kind of rock it is.

Each rock has a different energy signature, which we are able to know when our energy vortexes in our body are working and especially when we are in communication through our fibrous strands of the fascia. This is represented by the hand with nothing on it, which is in communication through the fascia because we have soul self entry. This gives us limitless information about the rock, maybe what was happening around it when it formed, how it got separated from where it formed, and how it came to be in our hand.

The soul begins its developmental journey into energetic form which becomes the complex container ultimately of soul essence. As the body develops these containers, energetic stages are either completed or not. If they are, a slow and gradual connection to soul essence begins. Once soul self entry has occurred, the soul essence will take its position in the third ventricle and be the first of the access points to develop that provide navigation within the abyss of the human field.

What We Create

An artist is hired to paint a picture of a castle and the surrounding landscape. The artist arrives and paints and paints, completing the picture. The painting is presented to the person who hired the artist. That person yells and screams and says, "where are all the pine trees, where are all the mountains in the background, where are the vineyards to the east or metal statues on eves of roofs?" The artist stands dumbfounded for on the days he painted he saw none of those things. He painted on days of dense fog! His painting, what he created, was limited to only what he could see.

We are limited in what we create, and the amount of information we take in. With this limited view we decode and then paint our canvas of life that we create daily.

Will we develop with the ability to interpret and communicate with all 5,000 signals before we create our canvas? Or, will we rush ahead on the 300 signals we can interpret, without our soul orientation, painting a canvas of life each day surrounded by dense fog?

Loss of Soul Orientation

Loss of soul orientation begins at our soul self entry as we do not develop our fibrous strands to aid in communication with the other 4,700 signals we receive each second.

Think of soul orientation as billions and billions of lenses to look through. When connected we are able to see all aspects through time and space. It takes a lot of work, but it is possible. Don't feel bad about yourself if you're not there! If you realize you are not on the soul orientation journey, this realization is the first cognitive step to Embodied Practice. You've just started!

These billions of lenses that all have soul orientation are represented by our simple example of the hand without the glove. Through your bare hand, you would see whatever happened to you. If someone told you about their life story, it would communicate through your soul orientation and you wouldn't get lost in their story. You would have your own soul essence communication, knowing if people were good, to ask for help for whatever you were seeking. If someone taught something, it would come through your soul essence connection of up to 5,000 signals and you wouldn't just simply believe it. You would know where you were and be in communication with your true self and the true self of others.

Purpose of Embodied Practice

I have dedicated my life to provide avenues for people so they can know from their developmental energetic connections. If people are the boxing glove or the baseball mitt examples, they can move on and become the bare hand and gain their soul orientation through soul self entry and Embodied Practice and the 13 Developmental Stages of Humans. Not that we wouldn't attach to some other teaching or some other awakening, as long as it was interpreted through our soul orientation and comes through that lens, instead of coming through the orientation of the religion, philosophy, or teacher. In Embodied Practice, the first thing awakened is one's soul essence sphere in the center of head. Then all that is taught after comes through or in communication with their own soul essence, this gives one communication with their true self as it is in the containers of the Healing and Focused Practice while building the structures which will ultimately house their complete soul essence.

Chapter 3

Creating Space for Embodied Healing

Begin soul essence activation in center of head

Emergence also has a point of origin. At the beginning of creation there was emergence. There was simply a contraction in and then a contraction out that has continued to take on more forms and more aspects than we can ever learn, know or understand in a billion lifetimes.

Beginning Healing Practice

Option 1: You can read through the book like any other, gathering all the sensing concepts and information, then return and do the Practice Segments and activations for each of the Embodied Practice Segments. Use the guided Embodied Practice Segments in this book to activate each part of the healing practice.

Option 2: You can read and stop at each Embodied Practice Segment and work with it for two to seven days. Then, read and move onto the next chapter and Practice Segment(s).

Option 3: Do the Practice Segments in each chapter first, then read the chapter.

Option 4: If taking a class is preferred, all classes are offered via webinars or through SoulOrientation.com.

Option 5: If you become overwhelmed with feelings in the practice, you can request an Embodied Healing through www.SensologyInstitute.com.

Safety Note:
The Embodied Practice Segments will be too overwhelming to the physical body if more than one of them is added per week. They are designed to be done one per week.

We begin our Soul Orientated Embodied journey, through the pages of this book and the sphere containers that were created for the book, activating and developing our mechanism of communication. To support the healing process on all levels, a practice healing is provided in written form in this book. In addition, each of the healings in this book is available for purchase in downloadable audio versions at www.SoulOrientation.com.

Whether you follow the Embodied Practice Segments within this book or practice via MP3 sound files, know you are in the Embodied containers of the practice forged by me within the electromagnetic field of Earth.

Creating a Space for Our Embodied Practice

Select a space in your home. Using the same space at first is helpful but not necessary. A chair is needed that is comfortable and offers support for the seated embodied posture outlined in the following pages. If you desire, you can place meaningful objects around you. Remember that these objects are symbols and that meaning only emerges from connection to soul essence.

Begin each Practice Segment with the settling pause of your exhale and the Four-Part Breath. Over time, comfort is achieved with the Four-Part Breath and the finger associations which are fully outlined in Chapter 7.

Position of Beginning Practice – Seated Structure of Practice

The first posture of practice is seated. We first begin sitting with the back supported in the chair or we can begin by sitting on the edge of the chair to situate the sit bones. It is best to use a straight-backed chair with a hard ridge, such as a folding chair. Place your feet flat and straight on the floor, middle toes line up with your knees, your legs are in a relaxed 90-degree angle, your hands are resting on your thighs with palms facing your lower belly, and place your shoulders in the spot they feel most relaxed.

Contract the core muscles in, pulling the belly button in towards the spine, while contracting the pelvic floor up and the belly button down into the center of your lower belly. When you are able to do this, the sacrum, or tail bone, moves down and forward. The femur heads will naturally rotate slightly inward (see figure below), which make it feel like the sacral area of the lower back is opening. The shoulders move back and down. Adjust the sternum back down. Exhale and allow the chest to relax down without rounding the shoulders - you are now in seated posture.

Example of Femur Heads Rotating In

Micro Body Shifts

As we are supported in seated practice and once we begin to open our energy channels, our fascia in our body will naturally want to make shifts. Understand this and allow your body to make micro-shifts.

The flow of water creates the riverbed. Similarly, the flow of energy in the body creates the open structure in the fascia so the fascia will hold a charge and vibration. An open structure is the physical ability of each the fascia strands to hold a charge and vibration such as the bare hand example and in communication with the unseen energy. As this occurs, we can work with micro-shifts in the body to allow the muscles, tendons, and fascia to create the riverbeds in the body, so to speak, that support our embodied soul as it develops. For example, if the shoulders feel tight during Embodied Practice, bring awareness to them. Ask them to micro-shift back and down. They will move slightly and the flow will continue to support. Moving the shoulders too far out and down will stop flow.

Practice Segment 01 - Awakening Soul Essence Sphere

This section leads you, step by step, to awaken your soul essence sphere, a pulsating sphere of golden hue at first, morphing in color over time. Your soul essence sphere is activated in the physical center of your head, the third ventricle of the brain. For new students, without the direct support of the Embodied teacher, we begin soul essence pulse activation in the aural center of the head. When your soul essence sphere is ready, it will drop into its physical space in the body, the center of your head or the "third ventricle".

To find the center of your head, place one finger between your eyebrows and one finger directly opposite it on back of your head. Draw an imaginary line between the two fingers. Leave the imaginary line in place. Now place one finger above each ear and draw another imaginary line between those two fingers. The intersection of the two lines is the center of the head. Six inches directly above, in our electromagnetic energy field, or aura, is the aural center of the head.

The center of your head is the space reserved for your soul essence sphere. No other energy besides your own, ever, belongs in the center of your head, or the aural center of your head. The pulsation of the soul essence sphere clears energy from others that does not belong there. It also begins to clear the underlying energy of any repetitive or intruding thoughts.

Seated Practice

Allow your head to come to a neutral position (not tilted forward or back).
Move back in the chair until your spine is physically supported by the back of the chair or a towel roll.
Place your feet flat and straight on the floor, legs in an L shape position.
Line up your knees with your hip bones.
Position your hands, resting on your thighs, so your shoulders feel most relaxed.
Pull your belly button towards the spine.
Pull up on the muscles of the pelvic floor, like kegel exercises.
Allow a slight tilt of the pelvic position that these contractions create.
Hold the position. Release the muscular tension if able.
Relax the sternum and shoulders once again, back down if able.
Allow your body to make micro-shifts as it settles into the practice.

Settling Breath
Exhale.
Pause. Connect fingerprint of the thumb to the fingerprint of the pinky in the pause after the exhale. (Settle into the pause, only as long as is comfortable for you, usually between one and five seconds, initially.)
Inhale. Release the thumb to pinky connection, and take a relaxed inhale.
Exhale.

Pause. Connect the fingerprints of the thumb and pinky.

Inhale. Release the thumb to pinky connection, relax and inhale.

Exhale.

Pause. Connect thumb to pinky in the pause after the exhale. Settle into the pause of the breath.

Inhale. Release the thumb to pinky connection. Relax and inhale when you are ready.

Exhale.

Pause. Settle into the pause of the breath, connect the fingerprints of the thumb and pinky finger.

Open to the pause, settling in.

Repeat this exercise four to five times.

Calling into Embodied Form of Soul Essence Sphere

Exhale.

Pause. In the pause of the exhale, allow yourself to connect with Earth in any way you are able.

Inhale. Relaxed inhale. Experience Earth.

Exhale.

Pause. Connect thumb to pinky in the pause of the breath.

Regular breath. Continue the breathing in any way that is comfortable for you.

Greet Mother Earth. Know that Earth remembers your soul essence.

Ask Earth to send a stream of energy upwards. In her remembrance of your soul essence she sends a red stream of energy, as thin as a thread of spider silk. Know, see, or sense this as it occurs.

The energy will gather in a sphere, no bigger than a large marble (¾ inch in diameter), 18 to 20 inches in front of you at the height of your nose. The sphere will pulsate like a heartbeat.

Regular breath. Be with your pulsing soul essence sphere as it continues to form. Use your regular breath for a minute or two - be with the formation of your soul essence sphere.

Exhale.

Pause. In the pause, connect thumb to pinky. Thank Earth for the remembrance of your soul essence.

Inhale. Release thumb from the pinky. The energy stream releases back into the Earth. The soul essence sphere remains at the height of your nose. Allow the sphere to pulsate in and pulsate out.

Exhale.

Pause. In the pause of the exhale, connect thumb to pinky. Know that your essence has taken form between Earth and Sky.

Inhale. Release the connection of the thumb and pinky.

Exhale. Settle into the pause of the breath, thumb connected to pinky finger. Greet Sky and the four layers of Earth's atmosphere.

Inhale.

Exhale.

Pause. Connect thumb to pinky finger. Ask Sky for a stream of energy to form and charge your soul essence sphere. As before, this energy stream will be as thin as a thread of spider silk.

Inhale. Release the thumb to pinky connection.

Exhale.

Pause. In the pause of the breath, the thread of sky energy will merge with the red sphere of Earth energy. It is a golden hue.

Inhale.

Regular breath. Give yourself permission to know, see or sense the right mix of Sky energy that is needed to create your unique soul essence sphere. As the energies merge, the sphere turns into the vibration and frequency of the color gold, your unique soul essence hue of gold. (If yours appears as a different color, allow it to be that color.) Thank Sky. The energy flow from Sky will release and your soul essence sphere will remain. Breathe however you can. Be with your sphere. Observe its brilliance, experience its pulse, and be aware of its energy. Take as long as you want. Know your position in the Universe between Earth and Sky. Stay with your sphere for three to six breaths.

Exhale.

Pause. Connect thumb to pinky in the pause of the breath. Be with your soul essence sphere in front of you. Be with your aural center of your head.

Inhale. Release thumb from pinky.

Exhale.

Pause. Connect thumb to pinky in the pause of the breath. Be with your soul essence sphere in front of you. Be with your aural center of your head.

Inhale. Release thumb from pinky.

Exhale.

Pause. Connect thumb to pinky in the pause of the breath. Be with your soul essence sphere in front of you. Be with your aural center of your head.

Inhale.

Regular breath. Allow your soul essence sphere to move into the aural center of your head.

This is located six inches above the physical center of your head. If the sphere does not seem ready to move positions, allow it to stay in front of you. It will move when it is ready. This could take a few days or a few weeks. Be with your essence and it will move into position.

Exhale. Connect thumb to pinky in the pause of the exhale.

Inhale. Release thumb from pinky.

Exhale. Soul essence sphere pulses in, ever gathering soul essence energy back to you.

Inhale. Soul essence sphere pulses out to meet.

Exhale. Soul essence sphere pulses in, ever gathering soul essence energy back to you.

Inhale. Soul essence pulses out to meet.

Exhale.

Pause. Connect thumb to pinky in the pause of the breath. Soul essence sphere pulses in, ever gathering soul essence back to you.

Stay with your soul essence pulse for two to three minutes or longer, if it feels good to come home. If grief comes up, know that it is the grief of joy.

Close Practice

Exhale. From your soul essence in the center, or aural center of the head, allow your soul essence sphere to begin contracting in, to the size of a grain of sand or a seed, whichever is more comfortable for you while not in active Embodied Practice.
Inhale. Inhale when you are ready.
Exhale. Soul essence contracts in. The sphere grows denser, but loses no soul essence as it contracts in.
Inhale. Inhale when you are ready.
Exhale. Soul essence contracts in.
Continue your soul essence pulsation, with or without connecting thumb to pinky, as you read these words. Take as many exhales as you need until your sphere is the size of a grain of sand or a seed. As your soul essence contracts down in size, no soul essence energy is lost.

Balancing Out Your Energy

Balance out any excess energy that may have built up during practice in the following way:
Relax all the muscles of the neck, allowing the head to droop down, nose pointing toward the floor.
Release the arms and hands so they also droop toward the floor.
One vertebra at a time, starting from the top one nearest the neck, release the vertebra as you bend the spine slowly down, hands moving toward the floor.
Open the palms up, facing the floor for most, or for some with the flexibility the palms will touch the floor. Release any excess energy that may have built up during practice.
Imagine a pulley between your shoulder blades and, when you are ready, imagine it pulling you up one vertebra at a time, starting from the vertebra closest to the tailbone.
Stack one vertebra on top of the other, as the pulley moves you slowly to an upright position.
Lastly, allow your neck to rest comfortably on the atlas, the top bone of the spine.

You have just completed the first activation healing of Embodied Practice. This healing reestablishes communication with your soul essence, the most important learning of Embodied Practice. This healing can be practiced again and again or can be practiced simply with the soul essence pulse as described at the end of healing.

For those of us that prefer to have a large road atlas view of where Embodied Practice is taking us, I have included the following. For those of you that prefer a turn-by-turn method, please skip to the next chapter.

Healing Practice

Begin in active healing practice or active practice. Our energetic development enables us to take in and interpret all of the 5,000 energetic signals coming to us at any moment. The interrelated Embodied Practice enables us to return to the state of being able to interpret all 5,000 signals at any given moment. This practice is provided in this book. These may be done once or many times, following the Practice Segments in the book or audio recordings on www.SoulOrientation.com. We set aside a quiet time and space to practice this daily.

Soul Orientation 24/7 Practice

Because we are meant to be in communication for 24 hours a day, 7 days a week, parts of this practice are meant to always be functioning. The aspects of our embodied orientation from this book, that are meant to be open for communication for 24 hours a day, 7 days a week, are the soul essence sphere and the grounding corridor.

Focused Practice

Focused practice is used until we reach completion of our energetic development. It is used to facilitate completion of The 13 Energetic Developmental Stages of Humans, past life footprint integration, and our energetic connection throughout all parts of our physical body and our vortex body.

Pulse Practice

When you feel ready to move to Pulse Practice, you can sign up for a webinar on SoulOrientation.com. Pulse Practice is complicated, yet ever healing – connecting us deeper and deeper to the pulse process across time and space.

Embodied Movement Practice

This is a different way of connecting to the elements in the fascia tracts, joints, and vortex column. We activate this practice in movement, such as exercise, wielding a staff, or moving in Universe in communication.

Chapter 4

Grounding

Grounding is a multi-faceted topic with many perspectives. Many people over the years have written about grounding. If a person acts wild and crazy, someone might say, "Oh, you need to get grounded", although they may not really know what they are saying. People talk about getting grounded in the physical stance of being connected through their feet. In addition, the field of psychology has taken many looks at grounding in terms of mental status.

In Embodied Practice, we have a different understanding of grounding; how it happens in our physical form and how our water connection gives us sensing information about who we are. You are now familiar with the center of your head. Soon you will learn about the grounding disc which connects to our still point in the flow of mantle in center of Earth. The grounding disc is the mechanism of connection to our still space and therefore to the flow of grounding.

Our grounding disc is located between the bottom of the bones of the sacrum and the top of the coccyx bone. Together with our soul essence sphere in the center of our head they create the points that our inner sense of self develops from, one of the three lines of our soul orientation.

Imagine a guitar string from the center of your head connected to the grounding disc running through the perfect center of each embodied vortex (discussed in later chapters). Each of the vortexes are activating, strumming the guitar string, and sending a vibration to the grounding disc. Our grounding disc puts this into Earth's language and sends it down the grounding corridor to our still point in the flow of mantle. Earth and water can respond, ever-adjusting our orientation or position. Think of the grounding disc where things are activated, such as how or where on the string it is strummed to make a sound from the vibration. The grounding disc is our secondary point of Embodied Orientation, one of the axis lines of orientation in the abyss of the human field.

Points of Orientation

The two points in space, the center of our head and our grounding to our still point in the flow of mantle, allow us to have a sense of our soul or a sense of ourselves within the core of our being. These two points allow us to reference our lives through a non-linear process.

For example, we receive a phone call from an unhappy person. Maybe they are at work and complain or are not happy with something. It could even be something we did or they just have bad news. Perhaps they are just saying something we don't particularly want to hear. In all of these situations, it is very easy to move outside of ourselves and lose that internal ability to feel who we are in the onslaught of this energy. The reasons for the phone call are all examples of field energy moving into our energy. How we relate to the situation and our ability to keep organized in our own body is significant to the daily quality of our lives.

To better understand some of the aspects of grounding, I want to share a story from many moons ago. So long ago, that it may as well have been a past life (although it was this one). I was 16 and I went on a wilderness adventure canoe trip with ten girls. The very first day out of the ten day journey, in the wilds of Canada, our guide disappeared. So, we were on our own to navigate. As the days went on, many poor decisions were made that put us in many difficult situations. One day, we decided it would be wonderful to cross a four mile lake under moonlight. We loaded up our canoes with all our gear, with three girls per canoe, and began paddling. Once we got to the center of the lake, out of nowhere (or so it felt to us) a storm ensued.

We were in very huge waves and in very heavy canoes. Now here is the example of a physical aspect of grounding; the waves were hitting the canoe and the canoe would not tip if the psoas muscles of each of us in the canoe were shifting with the waves. Our psoas muscle allows our body to shift with the rhythm of the waves. If our weight was met with the rhythm of the waves, the canoe would capsize. I realized that the two girls in my canoe were not going to be able to do this since they were terrorized with fear and their psoas muscle could not work.

This illustrates a mechanism of grounding in the physical ability to shift back and forth: to be with the waves by maintaining a connection with your body string within the core of your physical form. This aspect of grounding is also an energy connection to your soul essence which will help you make decisions beyond regular knowing.

I asked the girls that were in the canoe with me to lie down in the bottom of the canoe, which they gladly and immediately did. Next I went about figuring out how I was going to paddle to the shore. At this point we had lost the beautiful bright light of the moon reflecting on the lake. The sky was now pitch-black with lightning. Every time the lightning would strike it illuminated the sky, allowing me to get a bearing on the land. Only then would I adjust my paddle strokes to steer the canoe to shore.

This is the second mechanism that grounding allows us to do. We keep in contact with our internal sense even though it may not be constant. We have the ability to communicate with our soul essence because we know it is within us to wait and then act instead of just paddling like crazy without knowing where we would end up. That is how I and another canoe made it to shore.

The third canoe capsized. We were all standing on the shore and we could hear them yelling and could see them vaguely when the lightning flashed. Here was another decision to face: do we go back in the water or do we stay on shore? I decided to go back in the water with a canoe.

When I got to the girls they were hanging onto the capsized canoe. I found the canoe was too heavy to move in the water since their packs were tied down to the canoe. In their fear, the girls could not bring forth their ability to be with the rhythm of the waves. In energetic terms we would call this the abyss because they were in the dark amid the vast lake. Without physical sight they were not able to feel the rhythm of the waves in order to flip the canoe over at the right moment. Because of the heavy weight, it was not possible to flip the canoe against the waves; it has to be flipped with the waves.

I righted their canoe with the rhythm of the waves while they hung onto mine. After we got the canoe righted, one of the girls was too exhausted to get in the canoe. I had to go into the water and swim her back. At first, she fought me. The other two girls paddled for shore and reached land safely.

In our example of grounding, why did the girls – and why do so many others - lose their grounding? Many have not firmly established the connection in the center of their head or the connection to their still place in the flow of mantle, and have not had the life experience which has activated their four aspects of grounding through the aspects feminine, masculine, infinite, and finite.

In the storm of life, we may feel lost in the sea and are in a sense a victim or very vulnerable to having to be towed out or go with whatever meets us. Emphatically, this is about Embodied Practice. If we were using this strictly as an Embodied Practice, we would say that many things may swim by the girl in the lake who was exhausted. She was totally disoriented. If she would have had awakened soul orientation in the center of her head and was grounded to the still point in the flow of mantle, she would have known I was the aid she needed. In the sea or the abyss of life, many things swim by to offer to aid us. This is the beauty of grounding. In these very tough spots in our lives where we find ourselves in the dark abyss, without any knowing or ability to see within the darkness (which ultimately is an advanced skill), we want to grab onto whatever comes along – but then suddenly we find ourselves on a journey of something that ultimately is not our own or takes us where our soul essence would not.

Ground Dictates Purpose

Our lack of the mechanisms of grounding leaves us open and vulnerable to what or who swims by to tell us that they will save us from the abyss. We are particularly vulnerable to something higher, a "higher purpose" or "higher self." Without orientation, these offers only keep us in the linear disembodied state. Without our inner "guitar string" strummed by our embodied vortexes, we remain lost and wait to be saved. Only by communication with our soul essence do we complete our energetic development and fill our vortexes with our essence's unique crystal structure, allowing us to know if we want or need to be swum to shore by a distance swimmer and life guard.

Understanding How Fields Work: Electromagnetic Fields and Field Vortexes.

In 2006, Howard Johnson wrote a book, *The Secret World of Magnets*. It is easy to imagine this was the love of his life, to document this research of looking at magnets and describing it so very nicely. He talks about how when there's a north pole and a south pole that what had been observed for years was that iron filings simply made an arc much like kind of an oval arc around the north and south pole. Johnson's research demonstrated that an arc pattern occurs only if that which makes the arc is also magnetized. The iron filings around the magnet were becoming magnetized, thus only showing an arc shape.

Johnson was able to observe the magnetic fields in detail around a bar magnet (with a North and South Pole) and discovered that there are four vortexes, one at each corner. We can think of the center of our head as the north pole of a bar magnet (this is just an example - the center of our head is not the North Pole on a bar magnet!). Our still point in the flow of mantle represents the South Pole. We also have another interface which is our grounding disc. The grounding disc is between the poles, so we have four vortexes that are created electromagnetically, which are our grounding aspects.

The grounding disc combines four smaller vortexes joining in relationship, creating the grounding corridor - the mechanism of field connection and how we communicate with our still point in the flow of the mantle. This is how we stay grounded in communication no matter what hits us.

Each of these four smaller vortexes represents an aspect of life or being in body. One of the vortexes, the one to the left, represents the female, or our ability to form container. The masculine is to the right and represents the bringing of life. The finite is toward our back and that is our current experience. The infinite is to the front, and is our ability to emerge or to be with expansion. In other words, this is our ability to create change.

Four Aspects of Activation

In the book, *The Secret World of Magnets,* Howard Johnson explains there are four vortexes which form in an electromagnetic field. The nerve endings of the spine create the bio electric field that activates the four aspects of being in body, connecting to soul essence sphere and the still point in the flow of mantle.

The first aspect is feminine. We enter through the container of the womb, the feminine, and water.

The second aspect is the masculine, the element of Earth, and is on the right side. The first transition is for the soul to accept the body, which is the container of all that will be created.

The third aspect is the finite to the back with the element air. To fully be awakened we must transform from being water breathers to air breathers and understand light from being in communication through the unseen energy.

The fourth grounding position in the front of the body is the infinite with the element fire. To connect to infinite we must be able to communicate to change one thing to another.

Each of these aspects is connected through a process of awakening through pulse and allows a journey. The grounding disc is coded from what is in form with each aspect. The more we activate and use our grounding, the stronger it becomes.

Figure 1: Four Aspects of Grounding. This figure is a visual representation of the location of each of the four aspects of grounding on the grounding disk.

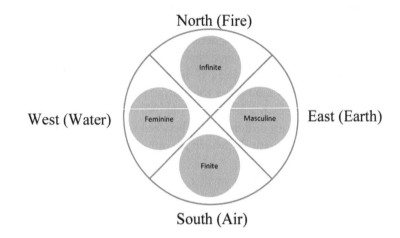

Practice Segment 02 - Embodied Grounding

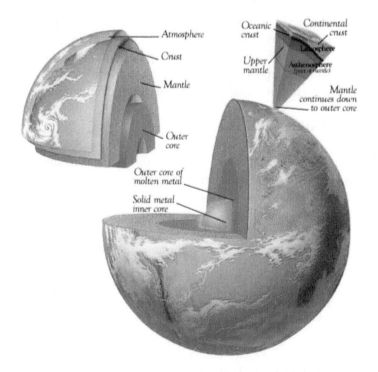

Grounding is first activated by creating the container of the grounding plate. Once the plate is activated, it is then used to activate the grounding corridor to the soul's point of orientation in space within your unique vortex in the still point in the mantle of Earth. The mantle is the layer between the crust and iron core of Earth. The movement of the mantle is the area of each grounding vortex, which is one of the mechanisms of communication our soul essence uses to orientate to the rest of the solar system and Universe.

Seated Practice Beginning

Sit supported and relaxed in your chair, legs at a right angle, knees in alignment with your feet. Your arms are relaxed on your lap with your hands facing up. Place your shoulders where they feel most relaxed. Adjust your head in a neutral position.

Exhale.
On the pause of the exhale, connect thumb to pinky, allowing your soul essence sphere to settle in the center of your head or your aural center of your head.
Inhale. Allow your soul essence sphere to pulsate out.
Exhale. Allow soul essence sphere to pulsate in.
Inhale. Allow soul essence sphere to pulsate out.
Exhale. Allow soul essence sphere to pulsate in.
Regular Breath.
Continue your soul essence sphere pulse until you feel settled.

Center of the Head Practice

Exhale.
Pause. Thumb to pinky. Be with soul essence sphere in the center of your head.
Inhale. Soul essence sphere in the center of your head pulses out to meet.
Exhale.
Inhale. Soul essence sphere continues to expand out till it reaches the size of a large marble (¾ inch in diameter).
Exhale. Soul essence sphere pulses in like a heartbeat.
Inhale. Soul essence sphere pulses out to meet.
Exhale. Soul essence sphere pulses in gathering its soul essence energy.
Inhale. Soul essence sphere pulses out to meet.
Continue soul essence pulse breath as long as you feel as you need to connect to your soul essence pulse in the center of your head (or aural center of your head).

(Note: This is a powerful soul self position practice that can be used in any life circumstance to gain functional support of ourselves.)

Regular Breath.
Imagine you have a DVD drawer on your lower abdomen. You push the drawer open. We insert the grounding disc (see Figure 1) which is like the DVD in four quadrants - we then close the drawer. The DVD is lined up in the center of your physical body at the tip of the coccyx, which is at the end bone of the spine.

From your soul essence pulse in the center of your head, greet the space of your grounding disc. Greet the left side of that space. From the center of your head, say hello to the aspect of the feminine, our point of origin entry aspect into physical form.
Exhale. On the pause of the exhale, connect thumb to pinky. Remember the journey.
Inhale. Release thumb from pinky, breathe in and experience.
Regular Breath. Be with your soul essence sphere and remember the feminine point of entry.

Continue for three to four breaths.

Clearing the Aspect of the Feminine

Exhale.
Pause. On the pause of the exhale, from the aural center of your head or physical center of head, greet the aspect of the feminine on the left side of your grounding disc. Ask for a droplet of green energy to come and clear it.
Regular Breath.
Imagine a dropper of pure green energy. Allow one drop to drop exactly in the center of the left side, in the aspect of the feminine. This corresponds to the left side of the body.
Ask from your physical (or aural) center of your head for that green energy to slowly pulsate out to no bigger than a large marble (¾ inch in diameter), and slowly pulse back into the size of the drop of energy.
Continue to allow the energy to clear until you feel complete for the day.
Using sensing and seeing, know what needs to be cleared. This could include grief, overwhelm or confusion about how you were mothered, etc. Let it clear. Clear what you are able to clear.

Clearing the Aspect of the Masculine

Regular Breath.
When you are ready, from the center of your head, greet the aspect on the right side of your grounding disc, the aspect of the masculine. Invite a dropper of red energy to come exactly to the center of the aspect of the masculine on your grounding disc on the right side.
Allow it to pulsate out the size of a large marble (¾ inch in diameter), clearing your connection to the aspect of the masculine, pulsating back into the size of a drop of energy.
Let the droplet of red energy pulse out clearing physical struggles, intrusive or elemental thoughts, clearing until you feel complete for the day.

Clearing the Aspect of the Finite

Regular Breath.
When you are ready, greet the aspect of the finite in the back of your grounding disc. Invite a drop of blue energy. Place it exactly in the center of the aspect of the finite, allowing it to pulse out to the size of a large marble (¾ inch in diameter). Clear any difficulty you have connecting and communicating with the aspect of the finite and life experience, pulsing back into the size of the drop of blue energy.
Allow every dot to pulse until you feel complete. Clear out fear of who you are, of what you could become, or grief of your essence creating a physical form to have life experience.

Clearing the Aspect of the Infinite

From your aural center of head or physical center of head greet the aspect of the infinite. Invite a dot of orange clearing energy to the aspect of the infinite in the front position of your grounding plate. Drop it in the exact center-aspect of the infinite. When you are ready, allow it to pulsate out to the size of a marble, clearing any fear of expression, or pulse process, or permission to have. Allow it to pulse back into the size of the dot of orange energy.

Allow the orange dot to pulse out to the size of the large marble (¾ inch in diameter) and back into the size of a drop of energy until you feel complete for the day. Clear out fear of not knowing the future or needing an outcome. Clear for one to two minutes.

Regular Breath.

Sit and be with your cleared grounding disc. When you feel ready continue to activate the four aspects, or (if it was a lot for you) do the closing practice and do activation another day.

Activating the Aspect of Feminine

Note: Activating the aspects is done with a different color than clearing. You would not wash your hair with hair spray and fix it with shampoo! Clearing and activating are two different things.

Exhale.

Pause of exhale be with your soul essence sphere.

Inhale.

Regular Breath.

When you are ready invite a droplet of blue energy to the left quadrant of your grounding disc, the aspect of feminine.

Allow it to pulsate out to the size of a large marble (¾ inch in diameter) and back to droplet, enlivening the aspect of feminine.

Regular Breath. Allow the blue droplet to pulse for one to two minutes.

Exhale.

Pause of exhale be with your soul essence sphere in aural center of your head or the physical center of head.

Regular Breath.

Aspect of Masculine

When you are ready, invite in a droplet of brown-orange energy to the right quadrant of your grounding disc, the aspect of the masculine.

Allow the droplet of brown-orange energy to pulsate out to size of a large marble (¾ inch in diameter) and back into a droplet. Enliven the aspect of the masculine.

Regular Breath.

Allow the brown-orange droplet to pulse for one to two minutes.

Exhale.

Pause of the exhale be with your soul essence sphere in aural center of your head or the physical center of your head.

Regular Breath.

Aspect of Finite

When you are ready, invite a droplet of yellow energy to the back quadrant, the aspect of the finite.

Regular Breath. Allow it to pulsate out to the size of large marble (¾ inch in diameter) and back to a droplet enlivening the aspect of finite.

Allow the yellow droplet to pulse for one to two minutes.

Exhale.

Pause of the exhale be with your soul essence sphere in aural center of your head or the physical center of head.

Inhale.

Regular Breath.

Aspect of Infinite

Exhale.

Pause.

When you are ready, invite a droplet of red to the front quadrant of the aspect of the infinite.

Regular Breath. Allow it to pulsate out to the size of a large marble (¾ inch in diameter) and back to the droplet. Enliven the aspect of the infinite.

Allow the red droplet to pulse for one to two minutes.

Exhale

Pause of exhale be with your grounding.

Regular Breath.

Allow the aspects - the feminine, masculine, finite, and infinite – to talk back and forth, back and forth. The feminine to the masculine, the masculine to the finite, the finite to the infinite, the infinite to the finite, the masculine to the feminine, the feminine to the finite, the finite to the masculine, the masculine to the infinite - talking over and over again, opening the grounding corridor to your still point in the flow of mantle.

Exhale.

Pause. Be with your soul essence sphere.

Inhale. Know your grounding. Corridor is open-release down it.

Regular Breath. Take one to two minutes to release any feelings emerging or feelings of being uncomfortable in the body. Stay in practice and release for two to three minutes, always with your soul essence sphere. Be with your soul essence pulse in aural center of your head or physical center of head. Continue to allow your four aspects to clear and talk.

Follow close practice in supplemental section. Balance out your energy.

Practice Segment 03 - Still Point in the flow of Mantle

Exhale.

Pause. Connect thumb to pinky.

Inhale. With soul essence sphere, pulses out like a heartbeat.

Pause. Hold in the fullness of breath.

Exhale. Soul essence sphere pulses in like heartbeat

Do this process three times.

Inhale. Awaken to your connection to the flow of mantle in Earth. Keep your awareness with your soul essence sphere in the center of your head or aural center. Do not go down into the mantle, you will get dizzy or nauseous.

Exhale.

Pause. Connect thumb to pinky. In the pause, find your still point in the flow of mantle in Earth. Connect to the still point in flow that only you connect to; the still space that came into being on the birth of your soul. From your soul essence pulse, ask for a dot of gold clearing energy to clear your still space in the mantle.

Regular Breath.

Have a conversation from the center of your head or aural center to the space that calls your name in the flow of mantle in Earth - your essence field connection.

Release any feelings down your grounding corridor. Take one to two minutes.

Close Practice

Exhale. From your soul essence in the center, or aural center of the head, allow your soul essence sphere to begin contracting in to the size of a grain of sand or a seed, whichever is more comfortable for you while not in active Embodied Practice.

Inhale. Inhale when you are ready.

Exhale. Soul essence contracts in. The sphere grows denser but loses no soul essence as it contracts in.

Inhale. Inhale when you are ready.

Exhale. Soul essence contracts in.

Continue your soul essence pulsation, with or without connecting thumb to pinky, as you read these words. Take as many exhales as you need until your sphere is the size of a grain of sand or a seed. We contract the soul essence sphere to a smaller size. When we contract the sphere down to the size of a grain of sand or seed we lose no soul essence energy.

Balancing out Your Energy

Balance out any excess energy that might have built up during practice in the following way:

Relax all the muscles of the neck, allowing the head to droop down, nose pointing toward the floor.

Release the arms and hands so they also droop toward the floor.

One vertebra at a time, starting from the top one, nearest the neck, release the vertebra as you bend the spine slowly down, hands moving toward the floor.

Open the palms up, facing the floor for most, or for some with the flexibility the palms will touch the floor. Release any excess energy that may have built up during practice.

Imagine a pulley between your shoulder blades, and when you are ready, imagine it pulling you up, one vertebra at a time, starting from the one closest to the tailbone.

Stack one vertebra on top of the other, as the pulley moves you slowly to an upright position.

Lastly, allow your neck to rest comfortably on the atlas, the top bone of the spine.

Embodied Practice

Embodied Practice is a 24/7 existence of soul orientation in the Dance of Reflective Relationship. Our soul essence sphere and grounding are 24/7 positions.

Focused Work for Grounding

Practice Segments 02 and 03 can also be done over and over. Work on clearing and activating the grounding disc until it becomes second nature to release energy down it and be in communication with the still point in the flow of mantle.

We have just awoken to a pulse connection with information that is held in the flow of Earth. These minerals and silicon particles that make up the molten lava flowing around the iron core were gathered together at the beginning of the formation of Earth. We are honored to reestablish the mechanism of connection.

To support yourself in practice, it is good to practice soul essence sphere pulse breath for two to five minutes every day to support your soul essence being in body.

See the Practice Segment Section for Soul Essence in the Center of your Head in the Supplemental Chapter.

Chapter 5

Container of Heart

"For everything that is, there is a container that brought it into being. For every container, there is something that creates it into being."

Kiera D. Laike, IRW

In Embodied Practice, our ability to create containers dictates, in part, our ability to monitor what is coming in and out of us and ultimately what is created in us. Our awakening to the understanding of our heart as a container and an organ which creates a container is established in soul orientation.

The heart is physically made of four chambers. Their functions are to contain and monitor blood flow. Rudolf Steiner's famous quote, "There is no difference between motor and sensory nerves, the heart is not a pump," can simply be accepted knowing that the pressure of blood velocity entering the heart is not significantly different from the blood velocity leaving the heart. The heart's four chambers contain the flow to the veins. The muscle structures of the veins, arteries, and capillaries circulate the blood. As the blood circulates through the veins, because it contains iron, it creates our bioelectric field, the aura or electromagnetic field of the heart.

This sounds simple enough - the heart is a container not a pump. Some may be saying, so what? When we see and label something with the wrong functions, then the true functions will elude us. Our heart is a container which supports our vascular system in creating our aural container. Through this field container we come into field association and ultimately reflective relationship (the Emergence Practice level and the third level of Embodied Practice).

Experiencing a reflective relationship is not possible without learning to hold and use a strong container of the heart. If we think of it as a pump we will approach it energetically as such. When we think the heart is a pump, this puts us in position of creating the electromagnetic field of the heart through force versus flow.

Electromagnetic Field of the Heart

Our heart field, in terms of understanding the functions of the aura, is too vast and complex to cover in this book, in Embodied Healing Practice. On the other hand, it's important to learn that the heart's aural field functions similarly to the electromagnetic field of Earth. The heart's aural field has a variety of layers, each with a unique function and purpose, which mirror the way the Earth's atmosphere works.

Field Association

Here I want to briefly introduce the concept of field association. Let us look at it first from a macro standpoint. The outside edge of the Earth's atmosphere or electromagnetic field interfaces with the electromagnetic field of the sun. In this field interchange, portals open up to create time portals. These videos can be found on YouTube at: http://www.youtube.com/watch?v=y3_vW5yrNek.

Field association occurs all the time with the outside edge of our auras. Our aura meets the fields of others we are with, in the room with, go to work with, etc. The outside edge of our electromagnetic field of our heart is also opening and closing to other fields it meets, when the conditions are right for portals to open and energy to transfer.

How Do Photons Affect How Electromagnetic Fields Interact?

Field transfer or field association must be understood through the mechanisms of transfer. A photon is a particle that carries light (and all other electromagnetic radiation). Light is carried over space by photons. Photons are responsible for electromagnetic force and are the force-carrying particles of electromagnetism. In general terms, electromagnetism contains information.

Because photons are the carriers and expressers of electromagnetic radiation (light, x-rays, gamma rays, etc.) and the exertions of electromagnetic force, they are the particles that express the force exerted by electromagnetic fields and sources. Therefore, any and all interaction between electromagnetic fields is carried by the exchange and interchange of photons.

All electromagnetic fields have infinite range. Their relative strengths diminish with the square of distance between sources or centers, just like the effects of gravity. This means that the further away the sources of two electromagnetic fields are, the less connection, communication, and affect they have on each other. But, because these fields are infinite in size, no matter how far away two objects are from one another, their electromagnetic fields are still connecting and communicating - a communication that is carried between them by photons.

Therefore, if we are in the presence of a stronger field, and we are not able to stop the field transfer, it will occur. In simple terms, we have all experienced being in a good mood, then talking to someone who is in a bad mood, and by the end of the conversation we are in a bad mood or vice versa. This is field transfer.

In the next chapter, we will begin to work with the outside edge of our aura, the electromagnetic field of our heart, using the Breath of Life to re-establish control over our individual field transfer.

Field Association on School of Thought

What happens when a million people pulse to something? Because of how our vortexes function coupled with the fact we are bioelectric beings, an electromagnetic field is created. This field facilitates or affects human development.

What Does This Mean?

Let us say one million people believe we create with our thoughts. This is not energetically true, but we can debate that another time. Through the experience of this book you will begin to understand that creating begins in a container. In 1952, the book, *The Power of Positive Thinking* was written, and over 20,000,000 copies have been sold. This book introduced the concept that the content monitoring of our thoughts and focus on positive thoughts can give us a positive outcome in life. Millions of psychologists used this book in their practice on their clients. It slowly fell by the wayside because clients were not able to outwardly monitor their thoughts. However, the number of people believing in this outward structure of monitoring thoughts created its own electric field within the human field. So people continued to believe it and presented the same concept over and over. This cascaded into a multitude of variations on the positive thinking theme which do not work.

The concept of positive thinking is simple thought monitoring. This is the process of telling oneself what to think from the outside in. Thought monitoring on its own will not yield the change we seek. People who get a result use numerous other tools, energetically and subconsciously, they are unaware of using. True positive thoughts are a neuropsychological expression of what is being experienced in the body; they come from within. If certain neurotransmitters or certain brain patterns are not present, one cannot monitor one's thoughts to become positive.

The belief of one million people in something creates its own field container in the human field. This affects everyone. Just as the field of the mass belief that "the world is the center of the Universe" held us back from understanding the Universe. Fields created on mass beliefs hold each of us back. For 20 years, I watched my clients struggle with the concept of thought monitoring. Every belief in something specific by a million people brings a container. Containers are ways of bringing something into form.

Think about having a container of a mass belief in the idea that "thought monitoring creates change". The health diagnosis of Obsessive Compulsive Disorder (OCD) includes a host of outside monitoring to bind anxiety. This cascades into depression, due to the fact that thought monitoring over-burns dopamine. Currently, humans in astonishing numbers are suffering from serotonin and dopamine imbalance.

Yet we continue to create in the electromagnetic field where we hold a belief that we can change our thoughts and then change our body experience.

Allow yourself permission to awaken to the mechanism of creation.

The Electromagnetic Field of the Heart

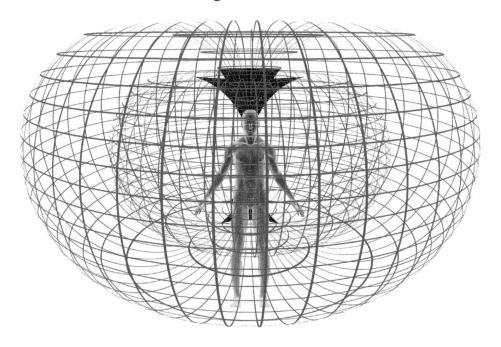

Electromagnetic Field Container Shapes

Dowsing Rod Too Far Forward

Since our electromagnetic field of the heart holds a charge, we can run dowsing rods through it and the rods will expand out to show us the shape of the electromagnetic field of our heart where we have lost our symmetry. For example, if rods ran over a person and they expanded outward in front, this would mean that the person cannot create. The heart would not provide a container for enough energy to be held within the system for creation. Think of it as if the gravity was very diffuse; in other words the container of Earth was a very diffuse container, less mass, less flow, less gravity from the flow. When oxygen began to be created, it would not be held within the container. More significantly, if oxygen had not been held here, then all the plants, animals, and humans would not have ultimately been created. For example, this person would get diagnosed from the psychological community as co-dependent. Their energy is going to aid or charge someone else.

Dowsing Rod Close in Back, Far in Front

If rods ran over a person and the rods were very far out front and close in the back, this means the person creates a schism or dualism and their container cannot balance. For this individual, things are over-created or under-created which creates instability in the system. For example, we might be overly helpful to someone and not at all helpful to ourselves.

Energy Field Side to Side

Looking at the container from side to side, this often shows our ability, our relationship to the aspects of the grounding, our balance within the aspects of the masculine and the feminine, with the yin and the yang.

Aura Size

When the electromagnetic field (aura) is too far out, it is too diffuse - this means there will be a lack of grounding, which creates an anxiety and inability to be in the present moment. The aura is too far forward and cannot be in connection with the aspect of the finite on the grounding disc. If the aura is too close, meaning too dense, this generally means there is no flow or a lack of flow and a lack of a space in which the person is able to feel or sense themselves. An example of this would be someone who is becoming very ill but they are not at all aware of it until they go to their doctor and perhaps they are diagnosed with a significant illness or cancer - even having symptoms for years and years, but nothing was addressed, because the sense of their self was so hampered by the too dense electromagnetic field of heart.

In Embodied Practice we hold an understanding of our electromagnetic field of our heart as a function of flow, container, and relationship in embodiment; these are ever expanding as we go deeper into our bodies.

Embodied Principle of Container

For everything that is, there is a container that brought it into being. For every container, there is something that brought it into being. This is kind of like a chicken or an egg, which came first? In Embodied knowing, the containers of the body reflect how they are maintained, activated and used. How containers reflect our being is key to our energetic development.

Examples of the mechanism of container are everywhere in life and science. Our cell membranes are containers that pulse and meet in the body, determining what the membranes let in and out of each cell. Soil is the container of all vegetation and a womb is the container of human life. Eggs are containers of life. One of my most favorite examples is the discovery of the container of space.

Space program experiments demonstrated that even in space there are unseen mechanisms of container which cause particles in space to clump together. Apollo 15, while orbiting the moon, used coffee grounds to document how coffee grounds in free-fall clump together. The coffee grounds organized themselves in bigger groups until gravity came into play. One of the clumps grew to a significant enough mass to have gravity over the other less clustered coffee grounds. This demonstrates space is a container in and of itself, because particles in space demonstrate the same qualities particles do in response to a container or field of gravity.

Container of Planet Earth

The flow of the magma, made up of molten minerals, flowing around the iron core of Earth provided the elements which are the container of Earth. It was this electromagnetic field that formed Earth billions of years ago. When the first lightning struck (which activated algae to grow) oxygen was produced that moved into the electromagnetic field created by the flow of magma. Without the flow of the magma around the iron core or the container that provides the electromagnetic field of the Earth, there would not have been lightning, algae, air, or the mechanism to contain the air when it was created by the algae. From within this container of Earth, all that we live and know has come into being. Our aural field mirrors this. It is one of the container fields.

Let's recap this chapter's Embodied Practice. We looked at our electromagnetic field of our heart, firstly, in a very similar way when we looked at the containers of Earth. It is produced by flow in the body - flow from the cardiovascular system and also electromagnetic flow within the neurons to other muscular and organ structures. The predominant field and structure is provided by the cardiovascular system – the heart, the veins, and the arteries. This provides our electromagnetic field or container which we refer to as our aura.

Practice Segment 04 - Electromagnetic Field of the Heart

Seated Practice Coming Into Position

Sit supported relaxed in your chair, legs at a right angle, hips and knees aligned in the "L" position. Arms relaxed on your lap, your hands up. Place your shoulders where they feel most relaxed. Rest your head in a neutral position.

General Center of the Head Practice

Exhale.
Pause. Connect thumb to pinky finger. Be with your soul essence sphere in center of your head.
Inhale. Soul essence sphere in the center of your head pulses out to meet.
Exhale.
Inhale. Soul essence sphere continues to expand out till it reaches the size of a large marble.
Exhale. Soul essence sphere pulses in like a heartbeat.
Inhale. Soul essence sphere pulses out to meet.
Exhale. Soul essence sphere pulses in gathering its soul essence energy.
Inhale. Soul essence sphere pulses out to meet.
Continue soul essence pulse breath as long as you feel as you need to, to connect to your soul essence pulse in the center of your head.

With Soul Essence

Exhale.
Pause. On the pause of the exhale, connect thumb to pinky.

Inhale when you are ready.

Exhale.

Pause. In the pause of the exhale, connect thumb to pinky. Be with your soul essence pulse in the aural center of your head or physical center of head.

Inhale when needed.

Regular Breath. Continue to be with your soul essence sphere.

Exhale.

Pause. In the pause of the exhale, connect thumb to pinky. Be with your soul essence sphere.

Inhale. Soul essence sphere in the aural center of your head pulsates out to size of a large marble.

Exhale.

Pause. In the pause of the exhale, connect thumb to pinky. Greet the soul essence sphere in the aural center of your head.

Inhale when you need to. As you inhale, continue to allow your soul essence sphere to expand to the size of a large marble.

Exhale. Allow your soul essence sphere to slowly pulsate in like a heartbeat.

Pause. Connect thumb to pinky finger. Be with your soul essence sphere in the physical or aural center of your head. Imagine snuggling into this safe space in the physical or aural center of your head.

Inhale when you need to. Soul essence sphere pulsates like a heartbeat out to meet.

Repeat for two to three breaths. Allow yourself to be nurtured by your soul essence.

Grounding

Exhale.

Pause. In the pause of the exhale, greet your four aspects of grounding. First greet the aspect of the feminine on the left side.

Regular Breath. As you greet the aspect of the feminine, be aware if it's in communication or out of communication. Ask through the center of your head, your soul essence sphere, for it to be in communication. If you need to clear it, do so with a gold pulsing droplet.

Exhale.

Pause. In the pause of the exhale, greet the grounding aspect of the masculine on the right side of your grounding disc. Ask for it to be in communication. If you need to clear it, do so with a gold pulsing droplet.

Regular Breath.

Exhale.

Pause. In the pause of the exhale, greet the aspect of the finite, which is the back position of the grounding disk, asking it to be in relationship. If you need to clear it, do so with a gold pulsing droplet.

Regular Breath.

Exhale.

Pause. In the pause of the exhale, greet the aspect of the infinite which is the front position of the grounding disk, asking it to be in relationship. If you need to clear it, do so with a gold pulsing droplet.

Inhale.

Exhale, when you are ready. Let your grounding corridor pulsate down in communication with your still point in the flow of mantle.

Exhale.

Electromagnetic Field of Heart

Exhale.

Pause. Connect thumb to pinky finger in the pause.

Inhale. Soul essence sphere pulsates out to meet like a heartbeat.

Exhale. Soul essence sphere pulses in like a heartbeat.

Pause. Soul essence sphere communicates to the center of your sternum.

Inhale.

Exhale.

Pause. Soul essence sphere asks center of sternum to clear.

Inhale.

Regular Breath. As your sternum clears, release down your grounding any feelings that keep your heart from charging its electromagnetic field, your aura. Continue to be with your soul essence pulse in the aural center or the physical center of your head. Release down and clear the sternum.

Exhale. Heart gathers energy.

Inhale. Heart charges electromagnetic field.

Do this breath pattern for one to two minutes.

Exhale.

Pause. Connect thumb to pinky finger. Sink into your sternum, electromagnetic field releases and balances.

Inhale. Release anything down your grounding corridor that prevents your electromagnetic field from balancing.

Exhale.

Pause. Connect thumb to pinky finger, sink into your sternum.

Inhale. Release downward.

Repeat this for two to six breaths.

Close Practice

Exhale. From your soul essence in the center, or aural center of the head, allow your soul essence sphere to begin contracting into the size of a grain of sand or a seed, whichever is more comfortable for you while not in active Embodied Practice.

Inhale. Inhale when you are ready.

Exhale. Soul essence contracts in. The sphere grows denser, but loses no soul essence as it contracts in.

Inhale. Inhale when you are ready.

Exhale. Soul essence contracts in.

Continue your soul essence pulsation, with or without connecting thumb to pinky, as you read these words. Take as many exhales as you need until your sphere is the size of a grain of sand or a seed. We contract the soul essence sphere to a smaller size. Contracting the sphere down to the size of a grain of sand or seed, we lose no soul essence energy.

Balancing Out Your Energy

Balance out any excess energy that may have built up during practice in the following way:

Relax all the muscles of the neck, allowing the head to droop down, nose pointing toward the floor.

Release the arms and hands so they also droop toward the floor.

One vertebra at a time, starting from the top one nearest the neck, release the vertebra as you bend the spine slowly down, hands moving toward the floor.

Open the palms up, facing the floor for most, or for some with the flexibility the palms will touch the floor. Release any excess energy that may have built up during practice.

Imagine a pulley between your shoulder blades, and when you are ready, imagine it pulling you up, one vertebra at a time, starting from the one closest to the tailbone.

Stack one vertebra on top of the other, as the pulley moves you slowly to an upright position.

Lastly, allow your neck to rest comfortably on the atlas, the top bone of the spine.

Chapter 6

The Breath of Life

Relationship's Function Outside of Electromagnetic Field of the Heart

Embodied Breath of Life is one of our energetic charging mechanisms in the body. The Breath of Life provides the line of field energy that contains the electromagnetic field of our heart, which is the field or space where portals are opened or closed for energy transfer.

Reverse Flow Power of Containers

I was sitting at a pool observing and enjoying two children playing with balloons and torpedoes. They threw the torpedoes in the water and the torpedoes would sink to the bottom of the pool. Then the children would dive for them. One of the children playing with the balloons got the idea that he wanted to put all the torpedoes into a balloon. So he talked his friend into it! They both worked diligently to get these torpedoes into a balloon and had no success. The balloon opening was about a quarter inch in diameter and the torpedo was three inches in diameter. Then, one child got a very good idea. He filled the balloon with water first. As he released water from the balloon, the other child pushed the torpedo into the balloon. Ah, success!

As the water flowed out of the balloon, the huge torpedo went in. This is how these two young children playing in the pool discovered *reverse flow dynamics* and created a simple example for us! This same mechanism is used in the Breath of Life. The torpedoes represent energy; larger energy that at first glance we think the balloon cannot hold. Yet, all the torpedoes ended up in the balloon. Actually, their biggest success was getting two large torpedoes and five medium sized torpedoes into the same balloon. That is quite a lot of matter inside the container of the balloon!

The outside of the balloon represents the membrane or container. Once it is filled with air or water it represents our charging in a different way, meaning the outside edge of our electromagnetic field. Like the balloon, if we are charged with the Breath of Life like the full balloon with water and torpedoes, then when a hand meets the balloon, the balloon responds back or has a way to come into relationship with it (opening and closing portals).

Here is a simple thought: if you had a blown up balloon in front of you right now and you pushed your hands on it, it would come into relationship with your hands. When you put pressure on the balloon, the balloon puts some pressure back on you. The balloon, unless you popped or injured it, would come into relationship. If the balloon had no air or water in it, the balloon would simply take on whatever shape you wanted.

Let's take this power of reverse flow example into embodied practice. Similar to when the children filled the balloon with water, the sacrum is first charged with energy in the middle of the sacral bone. This is done by the training of the diaphragm and intercostals of the ribs. We call them charging breaths. These breaths charge the sacrum. When we exhale, symbolized by releasing the water from the balloon, the cobalt energy of life comes in like the torpedo, unimaginably too large for the opening of the balloon.

This example has a positive correlation to the Breath of Life. We see the operation of reverse flow first filling the balloon with water similar to the breath; opening down the diaphragm and intercostals. Just as water provides the mechanism for the torpedoes to enter the balloon, charging breath and exhaling provides the mechanism for energy to enter. As water released, the torpedoes easily went into the balloon. The Breath of Life energy easily enters our body. This is the mechanism of the Breath of Life.

The next thing that I wanted to briefly mention, as we begin to discover who we are energetically, is the embryological development of the human form within the container of the uterus.

Three weeks after conception, pregnancy is in its fifth week (but it is three weeks after the sperm has met the egg). Three distinct layers or disks of cells have formed. These three layers go onto form different aspects of the structure of the body. The outer layer of the grouping ultimately develops into the brain, spinal cord and the skin as well as the outside container, and our hair, nails, and sweat glands. Then the middle layer develops into our bones and heart. The third layer develops into the endocrine system and organs. Looking at the outer layer of these three layers, we see that within our emergence into physical form we have a very clear energetic definition or example of how the inside (meaning the core), the brain, the spinal column, and the skin are one and the same. What is in the core is also outside. This is the Breath of Life.

Another complex example of this is acupuncture. There are many systems of acupuncture, but for this example we will assume that the outside layer, the skin, contains all the acupuncture meridians. There are also meridians in the core, which are comprised of the brain and spinal column. A predominant meridian in the core is the governor vessel. The governor vessel feeds energy to the meridians that are in the skin. This inter-relationship is being set up in the uterus three weeks after conception.

Even though I have been looking at these things for a long time, they still amaze and awe me. This awakening connects us to oneness of core and outside container as one.

Physical First Breath of Life

Our initial Breath of Life is a transitional breath of leaving the uterus and the moment our lungs stop breathing water and begin to take in air. The baby is moving down the birth canal and this process is not just like us sitting and telling ourselves we are going to take in air and blow it all out, and then just taking in a big breath. This moment is the activation of one of the sacred energetic things in the body. The baby is through the transition of birth and coming down the birth canal. The baby slowly releases water from the lungs while receiving oxygen from the umbilical cord. The slow conversion from breathing water to breathing air prevents the baby from needing to gasp for air. The moment of activation is a very slow process. As the baby fully comes out, the umbilical cord should not be cut to allow the baby to receive oxygen. This is when the baby starts preparing itself for its transitional breath and for awakening the charging of the breath in life in the sacrum. This is the beginning of charging the breath of the baby's container out of the womb.

What occurs, if it is not interfered with, is that the baby will be supported either in the arms or on the belly of the mother so they feel vestibular support in their core and on their skin. This support relaxes the baby's diaphragm. Our diaphragm is like a big umbrella or a big open balloon that is attached to the ribs. It is attached with tendons down on the inside of our body to our lumbar spine. Each baby waits until those tendons in the ribs relax; this, then, is the opening that initiates air flowing in. It is not forced in, it flows in. Breath of Life is, and it allows air to flow in.

On the baby's first exhale, the Breath of Life charge would come in and be present in the baby's sacrum at that very first breath. This activates the outer edge of the electromagnetic field of our heart.

The baby has its electromagnetic field but it is very vulnerable without the container of the Breath of Life. Let's go back to our balloon example and imagine the water inside the balloon is very vulnerable and precious. The balloon's shell, or rubber, is protecting that water. In the baby's case, the baby waits for Breath of Life to encase and hold it. Once the Breath of Life is charged in the baby, it can hold its field which communicates with everything else in the body and outside the body. The baby is waiting for this moment. Babies who are not given the opportunity to experience the transitional breath with the diaphragm and tendons releasing down, do not charge the outside of their aura and are energetically vulnerable. Don't worry, we will do a healing about this. Just because we missed this opportunity at birth does not mean that we cannot energetically get it now.

The Breath of Life charges in the sacrum which creates the container of the electromagnetic field of our heart that people can come into relationship through. Yet, there are many things that interfere with this transitional breath and the Breath of Life. One of these is if the mother is forced to have pain medication during labor. This pain medication goes into the baby and affects how the tendons of the diaphragm are signaled within the nerves in the brain stem. The other interference is when the umbilical cord is cut too soon. This puts the baby into shock and they are not prepared to take their breath. In this situation, when the umbilical cord is cut and the baby has not taken their first breath, they will immediately take it. They will not wait for the container with the water for this transfer of the reverse flow to happen where they can actually charge their sacrum.

Embodied Breath of Life

In the Breath of Life, the inhale creates the space. We wait to take the inhale, just like the baby is waiting, we wait in the pause of the breath. We wait in the pause of the breath and in that pause of the breath we want our tendons and diaphragm to begin to relax a little on their own. This relaxing of the tendons on the lumbar spine and the attachment to the ribs signal the breath differently and inhale is not forced - it flows.

When we practice a Breath of Life healing, or a charging, we do the three aspects of breath: the pause, the inhale and the exhale. The exhale is when that energy comes in charging the sacrum and then it moves out to the outside edge of your aura.

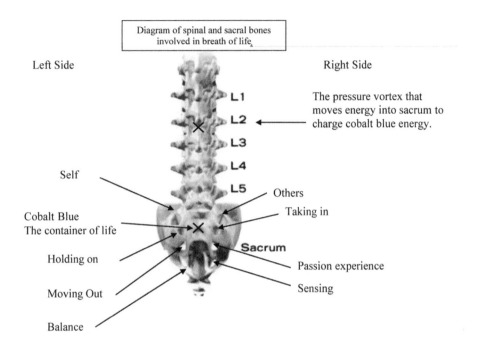

Diagram of spinal and sacral bones involved in breath of life.

Left Side

Right Side

L1

L2   The pressure vortex that moves energy into sacrum to charge cobalt blue energy.

L3

L4

Self   L5

Others

Taking in

Cobalt Blue
The container of life

Holding on   Sacrum

Passion experience

Sensing

Moving Out

Balance

Located at the bottom part of your sacrum is lumbar one through five. Lumbar 5 is the closest to your sacrum, which is the bottom bone of the spine. Right in between lumbar 2 and 3 is one of the main diaphragm tendons from the inside of the spine. This tendon is what the babies wait for to relax that diaphragm. When we inhale, that flow is coming down the tendons and releasing down. This releasing down creates little energy vortexes. Once the flow reaches the left side it has an inward swirl and on the right an outward swirl. Think of it like two little wheels pushing something down. This charges the middle of the sacrum.

We have eight spaces in our sacral bones and the charging space for the Breath of Life is the center of those, with two on the top and two on the bottom. On our exhale, with the energy we have activated, energy flow is like that water being pushed out of the balloon when the torpedo comes in. That is energy that we cannot force in, but the reverse flow allows it in. As we exhale that flow, that tendon pulls up and the flows reverse. It is in this reverse flow that we take in the energy of the Breath of Life.

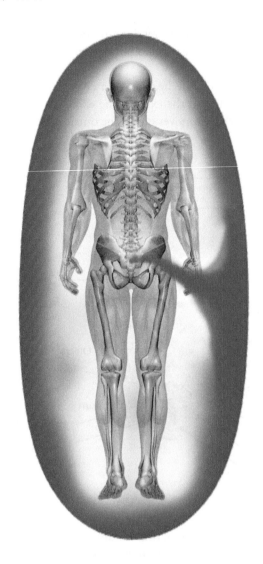

When we have charged our sacrum enough, this energy then moves out from our sacrum, out the back and coats the outside edge of the electromagnetic field of our heart which usually is anywhere from 15 to 20 inches outside the body. Any closer than 15 inches makes people feel very weak, pressured, and flighty. If we expand it further than 20 inches from our body, it can often make others around us uncomfortable. Optimum distance would be about 18 inches, but we do have a little bit of variance there.

Breath of Life

The layers of our auras charge from our back channels, supporting of life. The charge in the front is a return flow within our closed system.

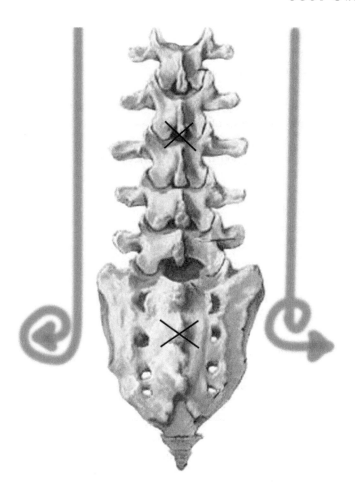

Practice Segment 05 - The Breath of Life

General Seated Practice coming into Position

Sit supported relaxed in your chair, legs at a right angle, knees level with hips. Arms relaxed on your lap, your hands up. Place your shoulders where they feel most relaxed. Rest your head in a neutral position.

Center of the Head Practice

Exhale.
Pause. Connect thumb to pinky finger, be with soul essence sphere in center of head.
Inhale. Soul essence sphere in the center of your head pulses out to meet.
Exhale.
Inhale. Soul essence sphere continues to expand out till it reaches the size of a large marble.
Exhale. Soul essence sphere pulses in like a heartbeat.
Inhale. Soul essence sphere pulses out to meet.
Exhale. Soul essence sphere pulses in gathering its soul essence energy.

Inhale. Soul essence sphere pulses out to meet.
Continue soul essence pulse breath as long as you feel you need to connect to your soul essence pulse in the center of your head.

(Note: This is a powerful soul self position practice that can be used in any life circumstance to gain functional support of ourselves.)

With Soul Essence

Exhale.
Pause. On the pause of the exhale, connect thumb to pinky.
Inhale when you are ready.
Exhale. On the pause of the exhale, connect thumb to pinky. In that pause, be with your soul essence pulse in the aural center of your head or physical center of head. Inhale when needed.
Regular Breath. Continue and be with your soul essence sphere.
Exhale. On the pause of the exhale, connect thumb to pinky. Be with your soul essence sphere.
Inhale. Soul essence sphere in the aural center of your head pulsates out to the size of a large marble.
Exhale. On the pause of the exhale, connect thumb to pinky. Still in the pause, greet the soul essence sphere in the aural center of your head.
Inhale when you need to. As you inhale, continue to allow your soul essence sphere to expand to the size of a large marble.
Exhale. Allow your soul essence sphere to slowly pulsate in like a heartbeat. Pause, thumb to pinky, being with your soul essence sphere in the aural center of your head, and imagine snuggling into this safe space in the aural center of your head.
Inhale when you need to. Soul essence sphere pulsates like a heartbeat out to meet.
Take 2 to 3 breaths and repeat. Allow yourself to be nurtured by your soul essence.

Grounding

Exhale.
Pause, in the pause of the exhale greet your four aspects of grounding. First greet the aspect of the feminine on the left side.
Regular Breath. As you greet the aspect of the feminine, be aware if it is in communication or out of communication and ask through the center of your head your soul essence sphere for it to be in communication.
Exhale and on the pause of the exhale say hello to the grounding aspect of the masculine on the right side of your grounding disc. Again, ask for it to be in communication.
Regular Breath.
Exhale.
Pause, on the pause of the exhale greet the aspect of the finite, which is the back position of the grounding disk, asking it to be in relationship.
Regular Breath.
Exhale.

Pause. In the pause of the exhale, greet the aspect of the infinite which is the front position of the grounding disk, asking it to be in relationship.

Inhale.

Exhaling when you're ready.

Grounding corridor pulsating down in communication with your still point in the flow of mantle

Exhale.

Electromagnetic Field of our Heart: Breath of Life

Exhale, as slowly as you are able.

Pause. As you come into the pause, allow your diaphragm to open (note: this will take awhile, until it happens in physical realm).

Inhale. Diaphragm releases down air and flows into the space of the lungs.

Exhale. Diaphragm releases up

Pause. Diaphragm prepares to open. Release down the grounding corridor tension, fears or other feelings. Diaphragm releases downward.

Inhale. As the diaphragm relaxes the sacrum begins to open to the Breath of Life energy.

Regular Breath. Do this sacrum opening breath for five to six times.

Exhale.

Inhale. Charge the space between lumbar two and three.

As the diaphragm relaxes down, the energy swirls to the left in an inward motion and to the right in an outward motion. Those two vortexes form in your middle lower back, pushing the energy of the Breath of Life down into your sacrum. The cobalt blue energy begins to charge into your sacrum.

Use soul essence sphere pulse breath if having trouble.

Exhale. On the pause of the exhale, connect thumb to pinky. Simply be with your soul essence pulse for a few breaths if you need, if able to let the Breath of Life happen.

Clearing of the Sacrum with Vortex

Exhale.

Pause. Connect thumb to pinky finger.

Regular Breath. From the center of your head, greet the two openings at the top most part your sacrum.

From the aural or physical center of your head, ask for the outwardly spiraling vortex from above and for the inwardly spiraling vortex from below, allowing them to meet. As they meet a clearing vortex will form.

This is a vortex that is ready to accept any energy that is ready to be cleared from those first two spots of your sacrum – of not being held or met by others. This might be early childhood memories or it could be in present moment with a spouse or friend.

Regular Breath. Take one to two minutes.

When you sense the clearing vortex is full with the energy from first two spaces of the sacrum, have the two lines meet. As the two lines meet, the outward spiral from above and the inward spiral from below completely meet at the vortex and their energy is no more or it will dissipate.

Exhale.
Pause. On the pause of the exhale, connect thumb to pinky. Be with your soul essence and with the two spaces which are second down from the top on your sacrum.
Inhale.
Take a few breaths, if you need to, to settle in while we clear and continue to charge the Breath of Life.
Exhale.
Pause. From the aural or physical center of your head, ask for an outwardly spiraling vortex from above and an inwardly spiraling vortex from below.
As they begin to meet, a clearing vortex will form that is ready to take in the energy from the second two holes of the sacrum – the energy of loss of permission, loss of the ability to be close, and to have what is needed.
Inhale.
Regular Breath. Take one to two minutes.
Use your grounding connection, if you need it, to help clear or release down any discomfort in the body.
When the second two openings of the sacrum are cleared, allow the upward line and downward line to meet, and the clearing vortex will be no more and transcend.

Greet yourself in the center of your head in your grounding. Be in communication to the sacred space in the center of earth, as we continue to charge the Breath of Life. Between the second and third lumbar spine, charge the energy flow - pushing it down into the sacrum, charging the cobalt blue energy of life.
From the center of your head, say hello to the third two openings on your sacrum.
Inhale.
Exhale.
Pause. Connect thumb to pinky finger. From the center of your head, ask for the energy spiral to come from above and inward spiral from below. As they meet, a clearing vortex will form. It will receive the energy that needs to be cleared from the two spaces that are third down on your sacrum.
Regular Breath.
Clear out any lack of affinity with experience. Clear any difficulty, sadness about what has been experienced in life - grief of loss of passion.
Exhale. On the pause of the exhale, connect thumb to pinky.
Allow yourself to settle into your soul essence sphere in center of head.
Regular Breath.
Finish clearing the third two spaces of the sacrum. Take one to two minutes. Allow the outward and inward spirals to meet and allow the clearing vortex to be no more and transcend.

Exhale.
Pause. Connect thumb to pinky finger.
From the aural or physical center of your head, greet the bottom two openings of the sacrum.

From the aural or physical center of your head, ask for the outwardly spiraling vortex from above and the inwardly spiraling vortex from below to come together. As they meet, the clearing vortex forms. This will attract the energy that needs to be cleared from the last two openings on the bottom of your sacrum - about overwhelm of the sensing systems in the body. You do not have to understand at this point what that means, the energy will clear anyway.

Regular Breath. Take one to two minutes.

When the last two openings are cleared of the sensing energy overwhelm, allow the two lines to meet, and the clearing vortex energy will be no more and transcend.

Exhale. In the pause of the breath, connect thumb to pinky. I am one in relationship.

Inhale. Connect thumb to ring finger. Open to the Breath of Life.

Slowly allow yourself to inhale, place pressure on your ring finger.

Allow that diaphragm to drop in the back, charging that space between the second and third lumbar spine.

In the pause of the fullness of breath, move thumb to middle finger, in communication streams out to the left inward spiral and to the right outward spiral.

Exhale, as you charge in the sacrum. Move thumb to index finger. Receive the Breath of Life.

Pause. Connect thumb to pinky finger. I am one in relationship.

Inhale. Connect thumb to ring finger. Open to Breath of Life. Charge the space between the second and third lumbar spine.

In the pause of the breath, middle finger, in communication swirling out, send the charging energy into the sacrum, charging the cobalt blue energy of life.

Exhale. Receive the Breath of Life.

Four Part Breath

Exhale.

Pause thumb to pinky. I am in relationship.

Inhale. Thumb to ring finger. Open to the Breath of Life.

Pause in the fullness of breath. Connect thumb to middle finger. Be in communication.

Exhale. Connect thumb to index finger. I am coming into relationship.

Do this five to ten times.

Close Practice

Exhale. From your soul essence in the center, or aural center of the head, allow your soul essence sphere to begin contracting into the size of a grain of sand or a seed, whichever is more comfortable for you while not in active embodied practice.

Inhale. Inhale when you are ready.

Exhale. Soul essence contracts in. The sphere grows denser but loses no soul essence as it contracts in.

Inhale. Inhale when you are ready.

Exhale. Soul essence contracts in.

Continue your soul essence pulsation, with or without connecting thumb to pinky, as you read these words. Take as many exhales as you need until your sphere is the size of a grain of sand or a seed. We contract the soul essence sphere to a smaller size. Contracting the sphere down to the size of a grain of sand or seed, we lose no soul essence energy.

Balancing Out Your Energy

Balance out any excess energy that may have built up during practice in the following way.

Relax all the muscles of the neck, allowing the head to droop down, nose pointing toward the floor.

Release the arms and hands so they also droop toward the floor.

One vertebra at a time, starting from the top one nearest the neck, release the vertebra as you bend the spine slowly down, hands moving toward the floor.

Open the palms up, facing the floor for most, or for those with flexibility of the palms touch the floor. Release any excess energy that may have built up during practice.

Imagine a pulley between your shoulder blades, and when you are ready, imagine it pulling you up, one vertebra at a time, starting from the one closest to the tailbone.

Stack one vertebra on top of the other, as the pulley moves you slowly to an upright position.

Lastly, allow your neck to rest comfortably on the atlas, the top bone of the spine.

Focused Practice to be done in active practice this week

Work as much as you are able with the Four-Part Breath and the four finger position. This will prepare for the understanding of the next chapter, Four-Part Breath.

Chapter 7

Four Part Breath

Evolution Connections of Breath

As we move into the Embodied Healing Practice we begin to work the first neural connection of the four parts of breath. Our four parts are mirrored and ever present in one of the Embodied Principles: 4x4 to Infinity. Let us, through our neural connection in human hands, join with four of our infinite ways of connection to the Universe.

When we connect our thumbs to our fingers within the Four-Part Breath practice, we use and activate neural muscular lines; these are the developmental power behind our neural activities. The neural muscular lines are in communication through the nerve fibers in the thoracic spinal column which communicate with different parts of the brain.

All human babies are born with the grasp reflex and we have all observed this at some moment in our lives even if we have never had children. If you put your finger in a baby's hand or rub something up against a baby's hand, perhaps a little toy or object, the baby's hand naturally closes around it. For most of us this is a very wondrous feeling to have a baby grasp onto our finger or to watch the baby grasp onto something, but we may not truly understand why. The origins and the beginning of the grasp reflex are present in the uterus 10 weeks after conception. The grasp reflex is there and the baby's hand responds to the environment of the uterus - one more example of moving into the abyss and then developing the physical mechanisms of connection to develop into reconnection through physical form.

For some of you this may seem amazing. Every time I teach this concept, I am still amazed by it. It is critical that this grasp reflex happens at 10 weeks. Let's step back for a moment to right before the soul essence reflects into the sperm and egg from the other side. At this point we have not chosen our situation in life or what exact things we are going to experience because we cannot know or see those. What we do choose is to take the life. We know on the other side that, when we choose to take or enter the life, we must lay down everything that we know on that side and enter the journey into the abyss, into our connection through the body. This is a process that begins once the soul essence communicates with the chromosomes and the baby's body begins to develop in the uterus. As the baby's body develops, each of these systems form: the arm buds, the spinal column, the brain bud, the heart starts working at seven weeks, the leg buds, the organs begin to differentiate at 10 weeks in addition to the little finger buds and this begins the grasp reflex. It is somewhere in these few days of the 10 weeks, as the baby's body differentiates, that communication with the soul essence can no longer occur. It is time for the journey of forming the soul in body which is the baby's journey to develop all the body's mechanisms of connection to soul essence through the soul-body. Once the body differentiates, we lose all communication of what we knew on a soul essence level and we enter into the journey of coming in through this new body. Here, we are on the energetic developmental journey - developing. We are creating and entering into a journey or learning again what we knew, or what we let go of. In Embodied Practice we call this "The Gathering of Inner Light", the pulse inward across time and space.

The grasp reflex is a key neurological occurrence and the final veil that closes us off from communication with our soul essence. Our journey of being in the abyss begins to develop a physical form. Later in the book, you will learn how to house soul essence and experience life through the body in physical form, not just organized photon light form.

After the baby is born, the grasp reflex is one of the primary reflexes that allow the baby to develop a sense of boundary. This boundary is critical in having a container in which to continue energetic development. These neural connections in our hands are necessary to begin to establish communication with the soul essence which, as we grow and develop, connects us to the Embodied 4x4 to Infinity Principle through the neurological connections in our hands.

We can see how important it is that we activate these important neurological mechanisms as we learn our Four-Part Breath. In this beginning practice, as with the baby, we are learning to create our own boundaries. Practicing the Four-Part Breath allows us to create our own energetic boundary and a stronger electromagnetic field of the heart, aiding the neural connections to be in communication with the soul essence on a clearer, deeper level.

A guiding principle in my work of Bio Self-Emergence is The Theory of Sensology; the understanding that humans are energetic developmental beings. This theory includes the 13 Energetic Stages of Humans. Each one of these stages is critical in each of us establishing our full connection through the body to once again be in communication with soul essence. Journey into Form: Soul Self-Entry is the first stage. This stage ends at three months of development out of the uterus, which is when the grasp reflex has allowed the baby to establish a boundary. The task that is called soul self-entry has completed. The soul essence can then begin its journey through the body, safe in its own energetic boundary to make its connections through the journey of the abyss.

Another important aspect that begins in this first developmental stage, Soul Self-Entry, is a bonding to the soul in the body. What I mean by this is that the soul essence has reflected into the forming body and an honoring of this must be present, an honoring that can only occur when the parents understand the soul essence reflection is developing as the body develops. The concepts of an old soul and a new soul have become quite widespread and popular in some circles. However, it is not quite the same as the parents meeting the baby and realizing that it is not only a bonding to the self, meaning in this physical form, which needs to occur. Instead, the body must be bonded to complete its task of developing a soul in body to once again connect with its soul essence. Bonding is the complete energetic process that occurs when the sensing systems are met with the truth of what is.

In Chapter 3, we learned about the center of our head and the gathering of our soul essence energy in the center of our head. Doing the Four-Part Breath, practice begins to prepare the center of the head (the third ventricle, the thalamus, and the hypothalamic-pituitary-axis) to become a good container for the soul essence energy that will create a self-sustaining soul essence sphere over years of practice.

Emotional Channels of Four-Part Breath

There is an emotional connection to each part of the Four-Part Breath. We initiate with our exhale, because beginning with the exhale puts us in a giving position or in our relationship position. We want to establish the rhythm of this beginning because it sets the stage for taking narcissism out of the human field. We may have opposable thumbs and a little bit bigger left and right brain hemispheres than other mammals but we are not as different as we like to think. However, we can be different in how we interface with the four aspects in the Embodied 4x4 to Infinity Principle, on a functional level. When we begin with our exhale, we establish relationship and then we meet in the pause of the exhale which is that space of the point of origin of creation, the pulsation inward.

In that space our body is increasing in carbon monoxide. This brings us into closer communication with plants and trees since they live on carbon monoxide. As we move into that space in our body, we come into a better relationship with them. For many of us, this brings up many feelings, for some fear, for some fear of being known, loss of control, and also for some a deep sadness. Basically, it could bring up any variety of feelings, including great joy – because most of us have been out of connection for so long that it is like coming home to be in pause.

This pause after the exhale (that we have been working with) is initiated with our thumb and after we exhaled all air out, we put our thumb print to our pinky print. Our fingers, given that they were originally part of the grasp reflex, are still associated and communicate with certain parts of our brain. Our pinky, from a neural connection, is most connected to the cerebellum. The cerebellum is kind of like a cauliflower at the back of our occipital ridge. It is mainly responsible for coordination of our muscles, posture equilibrium and connection. These are the function of, in a sense, knowing where the physical body is in time and space.

Here in the pause of the breath, connected to our pinky representing the cerebellum, which orients us in time and space, we begin to support ourselves and our orientation in yet another aspect. So far the aspects are our soul orientation in the center of our head, our grounded orientation through the four aspects of grounding: 1. Feminine, 2. Masculine, 3. Finite, and 4. Infinite. Now we have yet another orientation coming in when we are connecting to our pinky, communicating with our cerebellum in the pause of the exhale, in that space where we are in communication with something outside of ourselves and also inside of ourselves simultaneously.

Practice Segment 05 will begin healing on each of these aspects and the different feelings that come up. Then of course, after the pause of the exhale, we eventually have to take in air. In this taking in of air, the diaphragm releases downward and initiates the inhale, the way of the breath. When the diaphragm releases downward and initiates the inhale, the lungs move downward with it, and the air simply flows into opening lungs. Most people are all too anxious to inhale, and the air shouldn't have to push the diaphragm down, but we can and might have to force breath in. This difficulty in the diaphragm and with the inhale, with what we would call "taking in", is usually associated with a deep pain or sadness so the diaphragm does not release in an open and relaxed way.

Our finger neural connection, thumb to ring finger, supports the diaphragm in learning to release down and let the breath flow in. Our ring finger is associated with the limbic brain, the emotional part of the brain, or the midbrain. Those are three different names for the same part of the brain.

In this we can see, if we are taking in air and are having difficulty with our physical form and our fear or deep sadness about taking in, there may have been some events in which we were not met or we were not given what we needed. Hopefully we were given air, but it is represented in other physical things. This is very hard on the emotional brain. The midbrain surrounds the hypothalamus-pituitary-axis and third ventricle, our soul essence center of head, so you can see the significance of these connections. We work with the inhale, supporting ourselves with our thumb on our ring finger, allowing the inhale to become smooth and releasing any deep sadness down our grounding that we might have in every part of our Four-Part Breath practice.

The next part of our Four-Part Breath, our middle finger is associated what we call "in the fullness of breath." We move our thumb to our middle finger while holding in the fullness of breath. A higher percentage of people find this much more comfortable than the pause of the exhale. The fullness of breath is associated with the speech part of our brain and also the pre-motor cortex, which is involved in planning movement before we are even conscious about doing it. For example, if we were walking up the stairs while having a conversation with a friend we could see or glance at the stairs even without consciously thinking about what our body was going to have to do to climb those stairs. Our pre-motor cortex would plan for what was needed to walk up the stairs.

The feelings that can come up in this part of the breath, if you do not experience good ones, are usually deep feelings of missing the mark, or not being able to create or get what you want through your own skills and abilities. These feelings can lead to a deep anger or frustration. Fear of power or acceptance of your position in life can come up and can always be released down the grounding. Holding in the fullness of breath, meeting thumb and the middle finger, is associated with our creative energy. We create through our movement and therefore the preplanning of our movement is critical. We also create through our tone of our voice or our speech and so this is also critical. All of this comes together in one aspect of the breath in our practice, thumb to middle finger and holding in our fullness of breath, creating through container, not through thought monitoring.

The fourth aspect of the breath is the exhale. Our first exhale (at the beginning) initiated the pause and the first finger position. We began initiating with the exhale because it honors the relationship we are in with everything. By this time we have done the three finger positions, now we connect our thumb to our pointer finger. Our pointer finger is associated with the perception part of our brain, not entirely our pre-frontal lobe, but the part of our brain that determines and perceives – it makes decisions as to whether things are good or bad, etc. This is why, when there is an auto accident where there are three witnesses, they all have a different story because they all perceived it differently. They do not all have a different story in the sense that they made something up about what they saw. Each person perceived the events of the accident very differently. In Embodied Practice, we work toward perception in our interrelationship with being, or our relationship with everything, which is part of interpreting 5,000 signals a second. Embodied Practice aids us in a complete true perception, so we truly see what happened in the events of our lives – we truly see what is. When we obtain this true perception we make clear decisions about our lives or about what happened, thus creating change for pure life experience and only bringing into form what we came to experience.

Pulse First Beginning

Pulse is two things coming in relationship or meeting. In the Baum-Frampton Pulse Theory, the Universe is repeatedly expanding and contracting, pulsing in and out and back in again (until just prior to forming a singularity), forever. Observed during the Apollo 15 mission, coffee grounds experiments in zero gravity showed the grounds clumping together (coming into pulse relationship). Our ozone layer (that protects us) is in pulse relationship, sharing oxygen atoms. Each cell maintains our cells in pulse relationship with the rest of our body.

Pause of the Exhale

In the pause, we enter pulse relationship. So, we connect and coordinate with the space of the Universe in the pause aided by our neural connection, thumb to pinky. This begins a neural connection to the cerebellum, which links smooth movements, the opposite of trembling and un-coordinated movements. In embodied understanding of energetic development of humans, this correlates to the Soul Self-Entry stage or what our core sense of self will become to our relationship to self.

Inhale

Inhale is associated to the aspect of the crystal structures in the Embodied 4x4 to Infinity Principle. The inhale represents us taking in energy which supports the body in structuring its soul essence crystal structures. The neural connection of the inhale is through the finger position of the thumbprint being pressed to the ring fingerprint, representing the second Energetic Developmental Stage of Humans, Taking Form and Being Met. When we take form and meet then something else is created.

This connection supports our midbrain connection and our relationship to others in life.

Pause of Inhale Journey

The journey is what gets put into action by the structure that came from pulse. Earth's particles clustered and created its own gravity and its own field atmosphere. Hence everything created since is part of the journey, so humans are part of Earth's journey.

This journey is so multi-leveled that it is hard to have a good simple example. The journey begins in the pause of inhale. The journey is everything which happens once something occurs. You leave your driveway to go on vacation – what happens after leaving the driveway is the journey. The neural connection in the pause of the fullness of breath is then to the middle finger.

This neural connection is associated with Brocas Pre-motor Cortex, which is responsible for the planning and integrating of movement. It is clear, if we think our way through the journey on a cognitive brain level, we will forever be lost. This neural connection integrates our planned movements to our creative energy of flow.

Exhaling Reflections

Everything that has been created in some way reflects what it has been created in. A large scale example of this is, 90% of the cosmic sea is dark energy and 90% of our brain and nervous system is dark energy. Dark energy is matter with certain properties that have yet to be determined by science. Despite the lack of definition, we know that the Universe is 90% dark energy and so are our brains. Our vortexes shape our reflection of the four layers of the space time vortexes.

While exhaling, we meet back or are in pulse relationship. This is associated with the aspect of reflection in the Embodied 4x4 to Infinity Principle. Because we have begun to come into relationship, moved and created, when we exhale, we have something in our breath that meets back – if we exhale without these connections, our breath is empty – like someone speaking a lie. The neural connection of the exhale is through the finger position of the thumbprint being pressed to the pointer fingerprint. It represents how we take in life, our perceptions, and ultimately if we will be able to gather our soul essence.

Thumb

The neural connection of the thumb is also significant because we use it to activate the neural connections of the other fingers. The thumb's neural connection represents sensory memory, and the prefrontal cortex. In using the Four-Part Breath to activate on both hands, we forever have our prefrontal lobe, the part of the brain that ultimately forms the perceptions, in balance with the Embodied 4x4 to Infinity Principle, the back bone of creation.

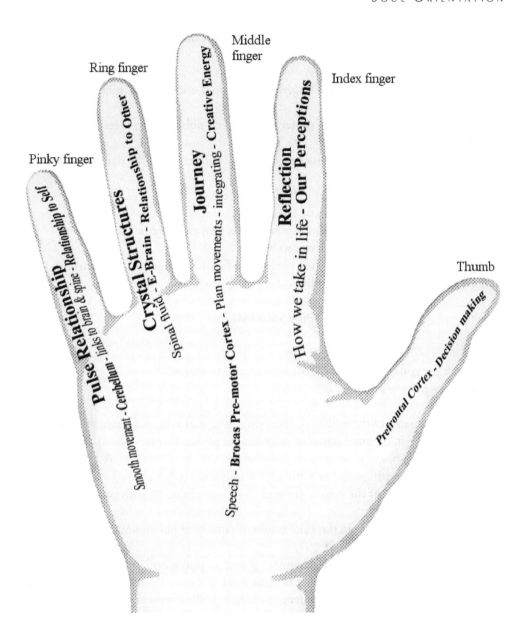

Pinky finger

Ring finger

Middle finger

Index finger

Thumb

Pulse Relationship - links to brain & spine - Relationship to Self

Smooth movement - Cerebellum

Crystal Structures – E-Brain - Relationship to Other

Spinal fluid

Journey – Creative Energy

Spinal fluid - Plan movements - integrating - Creative Energy

Journey – Creative Energy

Speech - **Brocas Pre-motor Cortex** - Plan movements - integrating - Creative Energy

Reflection

How we take in life - **Our Perceptions**

Prefrontal Cortex - Decision making

Practice Segment 06 - Four Part Breath

General Seated Practice - Coming into Position

Sit supported relaxed in your chair, legs at a right angle, hips and knees straight out from hip bones, arms relaxed on your lap, your hands up. Place your shoulders where they feel most relaxed. Rest your head in a neutral position.

Center of the Head Practice

Exhale.

Pause. Connect thumb to pinky finger. Be with your soul essence sphere in aural or physical center of head.

Inhale. Soul essence sphere in the center of your head pulses out to meet.

Exhale.

Inhale. Soul essence sphere continues to expand out till it reaches the size of a large marble.

Exhale. Soul essence sphere pulses in like a heartbeat.

Inhale. Soul essence sphere pulses out to meet.

Exhale. Soul essence sphere pulses in gathering its soul essence energy.

Inhale. Soul essence sphere pulses out to meet.

Continue soul essence pulse breath as long as you feel as you need to, to connect to your soul essence pulse in the aural or physical center of your head.

With Soul Essence

Exhale.

Pause. On the pause of the exhale, connect thumb to pinky.

Inhale when you are ready.

Exhale.

Pause. On the pause of the exhale, connect thumb to pinky. In that pause, be with your soul essence pulse in the aural center of your head or physical center of head. Inhale when needed.

Regular breath. Continue and be with your soul essence sphere.

Exhale. On the pause of the exhale, connect thumb to pinky. Be with your soul essence sphere.

Inhale. Soul essence sphere in the aural center of your head pulsates out to size of a large marble.

Exhale. On the pause of the exhale, connect thumb to pinky. Still in the pause, greet the soul essence sphere in the aural center of your head.

Inhale when you need to. As you inhale, continue to allow your soul essence sphere to expand out to the size of a large marble.

Exhale. Allow your soul essence sphere to slowly pulsate in like a heartbeat.

Pause. Connect thumb to pinky finger. Be with your soul essence sphere in the aural center of your head. Imagine snuggling into this safe space in the aural or physical center of your head.

Inhale, when you need to. Soul essence sphere pulsates out to meet, like a heartbeat.

Repeat last breath pattern with soul essence pulse, for three to four breaths. Allow yourself to be nurtured by your soul essence.

Grounding

Exhale.

Pause. In the pause of the exhale, greet your four aspects of grounding. First greet the aspect of the feminine on the left side.

Inhale. Greet the aspect of the feminine. Be aware if it is in communication or out of communication and ask, through the center of your head from your soul essence sphere, for it to be in communication.

Exhale.

Pause. In the pause of the exhale, greet the grounding aspect of the masculine on the right side of your grounding disc. Ask for it to be in communication.

Inhale.

Exhale.

Pause. In the pause of the exhale, greet the aspect of the finite, which is the back position of the grounding disc, and ask it to be in relationship.

Inhale.

Exhale.

Pause. In the pause of the exhale, greet the aspect of the infinite which is the front position of the grounding disc, and ask it to be in relationship.

Inhale.

Exhale, when ready.

Grounding corridor pulsates downward, in communication with your still point in the flow of mantle.

Exhale.

Aural Opening

Inhale. Breathe into the sternum, opening.

Exhale. Let the sternum relax down and a little bit back.

Inhale. Allow your sternum to open.

Exhale. Sternum relaxes down and back.

Continue these focused sternum breaths for three to four minutes or until you feel contained in your own electromagnetic field of your heart.

Breath of Life

Exhale.

Inhale. Breath of Life. Allow yourself to slowly inhale.

Exhale. Slowly.

Inhale. As your breath slowly relaxes in, allow the back of your diaphragm to come down with your breath, breathing into the back. Imagine it going down, adjust if you need to, hitting that spot in between lumbar two and three.

Exhale, each time breathing in, thinking of the diaphragm, relaxing down and charging the space between lumbar two and three.

As the diaphragm relaxes down, the energy swirls to the left in an inward motion and to the right in an outward motion. Those two vortexes form in your middle lower back, moving the energy of the Breath of Life down into your sacrum. The cobalt blue energy begins to charge into your sacrum.

Inhale.

Exhale. On the pause of the exhale, connect thumb to pinky. Count five seconds.

Inhale. Count five seconds.

Relaxed exhale. Count five seconds.

Pause. In the pause of the exhale, connect thumb to pinky. Count five seconds.
Continue this pattern until you have done 15 to 20 breaths, holding between five to eight seconds on each part of the breath.

Four-Part Breath

Be With your soul essence sphere in the aural or physical center of your head.
Exhale. Connect thumb to pinky finger. "I am one in relationship."
Inhale. Connect thumb to ring finger. Open to the Breath of Life.
Pause. In the fullness of breath, connect thumb to middle finger. Be in communication.
Exhale. Connect thumb to index finger. Come into relationship with the Breath of Life.
Continue in the rhythm of the Four-Part Breath for 8 to 12 breaths. During the process, if needed, release any feelings or tension in your body down your grounding corridor into the flow of mantle.

Close Practice

Exhale. From your soul essence in the center, or aural center of the head, allow your soul essence sphere to begin contracting into the size of a grain of sand or a seed, whichever is more comfortable for you while not in active Embodied Practice.
Inhale. Inhale when you are ready.
Exhale. Soul essence contracts in. The sphere grows denser, but loses no soul essence as it contracts in.
Inhale. Inhale when you are ready.
Exhale. Soul essence contracts in.
Continue your soul essence pulsation, with or without connecting thumb to pinky, as you read these words. Take as many exhales as you need until your sphere is the size of a grain of sand or a seed. We contract the soul essence sphere to a smaller size. Contracting the sphere down to the size of a grain of sand or seed, we lose no soul essence energy.

Balancing Out Your Energy

Balance out any excess energy that may have built up during practice in the following way:
Relax all the muscles of the neck, allowing the head to droop down, nose pointing toward the floor.
Release the arms and hands so they also droop toward the floor.
One vertebra at a time, starting from the top one, nearest the neck, release the vertebra as you bend the spine slowly down, hands moving toward the floor.
Open the palms up, facing the floor for most, or for some with the flexibility the palms will touch the floor. Release any excess energy that may have built up during practice.
Imagine a pulley between your shoulder blades, and when you are ready, imagine it pulling you up, one vertebra at a time, starting from the one closest to the tailbone.
Stack one vertebra on top of the other, as the pulley moves you slowly to an upright position.
Lastly, allow your neck to rest comfortably on the atlas, the top bone of the spine.

Focus Work

Practice the Four-Part Breath with the finger associations and the cognitive anchors (see The Four-Part Breath section of this Practice Segment). Work with this until you can stay in each part of the breath comfortably for 10-15 seconds.

Chapter 8

Earth Iron Flow

Embodied Principle of Flow

To get an idea of what flow means, I ask simple questions. If you could talk to a person that was here, who witnessed everything as our solar system formed, would you be interested in talking to that person? Would you feel that person would have valuable information about Earth, our solar system, and about what we may or may not want to bring into being? How would our lives or our very evolution change, if we were able, from an energy (photon light) transfer mechanism, to be in communication with all that had come before?

To further emphasize the power of flow, let's take a look at the vast complexity of our body. This gives us the perspective of the large amount of information we can connect to through a physical mechanism to meet and experience energy information exchange.

Scientists calculated that 9.1 billion years after the pulse contraction inward, or the beginning of consciousness in the Universe, our sun began to form. It took 50 million years after the initial contraction inward before the sun became a star. Some of the matter that was still within its sphere of influence (which is now our solar system) became Earth.

The person that we talk to would have witnessed the creation of our sun. This person is becoming more and more interesting as we move along the timeline. 150 million years after the creation of our sun, Earth was created (based upon evidence of the first rocks being formed on Earth). In other words, 150 million years after the forming of the sun (the sun becoming a star), Earth took shape and was formed. After Earth was formed, 750 million years later, we have record of the first life on Earth, bacteria. Moving forward, through huge amounts of time, 4.5 billion years after the sun was created, we have today. To put it in perspective of human lives lived, if the person we were asking the questions of were alive today, they would have lived about 47.4 million lifetimes, with an average of 75 years per life (and 20 years off between lives). This would be quite a journey and (within that journey) there is a vast amount of information to be learned. Within the elements of Earth, Earth itself holds all of this information. The trick, or the excitement, is in the development of our ability that is given to us through evolution to be in communication with this energy, or this vast amount of information.

As we begin to work with Earth flow energy, we begin to realize our own evolution from this huge perspective across time. In Embodied Practice, we learn about gathering our information through our past life footprints in creation and (when we add Earth energy flow) we are talking about adding to that 47.4 million lifetimes of gathering information that Earth energy has witnessed and gathered throughout the forming of the solar system.

Moving forward in time, just to add a bit of forward looking perspective, scientists have predicted that 1.5 billion years from now, the sun will start to undergo a new transformation and begin to de-organize. In other words, it will move toward becoming a white dwarf. If we look at how many lifetimes from now until that transformation of the sun, it would be 15.8 million lifetimes to live and experience life here and work through our energetic evolution.

To aid us in awakening to the possibilities that lie ahead for us in gathering our soul lives and emerging as energetic beings, we will compare the number of lives our soul essence may have created since the Genus Homo, including modern humans and their close relatives, emerged.

| 2.5 million years of humanity | 2013 | 1.5 billion years – sun becomes white dwarf |
| (26,337 lifetimes) | | (15.8 million lifetimes) |

We are just on the verge of our human energetic evolution. Our ability to come into communication depends on what will emerge for us through our ability to regain connection with our soul essence. Once we communicate to our soul essence, our sun has given us the time and space to possibly create 15.8 million more lifetimes and therefore, footprints, to aid us in gathering to our ultimate energetic evolution.

This may bring a little perspective, and some humility of the importance of why we would want to begin to listen, or learn the mechanism of listening, to Earth energy or Earth flow as we walk our path here on Earth. Remember that Earth sits in a space-time vortex within the fabric of the space-time container mirrored in the vortexes that develop in us when we honor our energetic development. Without the development of our vortexes, we cannot know who we are.

Coming into Flow with Earth Iron Energy

Before we continue, I want to recap flow. Flow has become a popular word, like many words that come in and out of popularity. I summarized the lifetime calculations so we could begin to understand what flow really means. Flow is the ability to have that connection across a broad spectrum of information and time. It cannot be flow unless it is across a very large span of things. I should not say that I am in flow if I was only able to stay connected within two minutes of something. That's not flow. That's staying connected within two minutes!

Next time you hear someone use "flow", in a popular sense, ask yourself in what context are they talking about flow and what there are the parameters of flow. Here, in terms of our Earth iron flow connection, flow means being in connection from the beginning of our solar system.

Within our physical form, we have the mechanism to be in contact with different aspects of Earth iron energy. In Embodied Practice, we start with Earth iron energy because Earth iron energy is the core and it runs in the bone marrow of our legs, our hips and then down our grounding corridor. It provides us with a charge, a container of information, and also a building up of our energy within our blood. This is just like the iron swirling around in the center of Earth which gives Earth its ability to meet the field of the sun and to co-create its own field.

When we do the Feet Vortexes Embodied Practice segment in just a little bit, we will begin with our feet. For some, the concept of feet vortexes may be a new concept. We have many vortexes in our feet that are able to take in energy and transfer energy, but we have one main foot vortex on each foot. It is located in the middle, right in front of your heel pad. If you place your finger on the space in front of your heel pad towards the middle of your foot, you will feel a corridor. This corridor is where three bones of your foot meet and create the space that is our foot vortex.

The feet vortexes, like all of our Embodied Relationship vortexes, have the ability to pulse down and open. This is what we will begin to practice. The pulsing down and opening is how we connect with Earth iron energy and invite it into our bone marrow. This occurs through what we call field transfer. Only Earth iron energy is ever run in our bone marrow. This is because our bone marrow is a very unique tissue and in certain aspects produces our red and white blood cells. There are three types of bone marrow: red bone marrow, yellow bone marrow, and spongy bone marrow. All of these types of bone marrow run Earth iron energy. In general, our red marrow is in our femur head, the butterfly bone of our pelvis, and our sternum. These are the four bones within our body where our blood is created.

Earth Iron Energy Flow Structures

Our femur head and the butterfly bone of the pelvis contain the largest portion of bone marrow. For the beginner in Embodied Practice, the flow of Earth iron energy supports us in opening to the charged posture of the practice of femur heads rotated outward. The rotation outward of the femur heads supports us deeper in the sacral area and in the charging of the Breath of Life.

Structure and Function

Our pelvis has the ability for lateral movement, meaning moving right or left. There are two positions. We have a frontward movement and we have a backward movement. Then we also have abduction, meaning rotating in, that we learned in charging the Breath of Life. The muscles of the pelvis are involved in these movements.

The *psoas muscle* is predominantly involved in our ability to move forward. This muscle is on either side of our spinal cord, on the bottom, and it hooks down through our pelvis bone onto our femur. The psoas muscle propels us if we lift our leg up and are stepping forward.

Then we have our *gluteus minimus*, which are the smaller butt muscles. They connect to the hip and this is what allows that abduction, better known as movement to the inside. The movement is an internal rotation of the thigh.

Then there is the *gluteus medius,* which is the larger muscle in the buttocks. When we are moving or taking a step there is actually a little backward movement before we move forward. This is what gives us our gait and propels us through life.

Of course, we also use the *gluteus maximus*, which is involved in some way in all of the four movements of the leg.[2]

Going back to understanding within the physical structure of the femur head and the butterfly bone of the pelvis: in this position in life and in Embodied Practice, we consider the joint of the hip and the femur head to be representative of our position, the "Position of Humans" we call it. This is literally our stance. It is our evolutionary perspective because we are upward beings. This position evolved to be in communication with Earth's energy.

Think of it as if we were flying an airplane, driving a boat, or even a car. We had no idea of what we should do or where we should go. Yet, we would constantly have a little whisper saying, "A little bit to the right…a little bit to the left…forward…back…right…forward…back" in communication with us. Soon we would settle into the whisper's instructions and learn very quickly we could trust them. This is a very simple and crude example of a very complicated thing; information about the human position on Earth through connection to Earth iron flow.

When we are in communication with our Earth iron energy through our bone marrow, through the production of our red blood cells, and through those structures involved in our position of life as we walk and move, it is as if the little whisper in our ear has been there from the beginning of the forming of our solar system. The source of the little whisper has witnessed the birth of the sun and understands why Jupiter decided to set his position up to protect the Earth from the majority of asteroids that come from the Oort cloud. Jupiter gets pummeled because of its position and not us! The whispering to you continues as you move through life and you have the opportunity to take guidance. I think that most of us would want to sign up for it. If you do not, that is okay too, but you would be missing out on billions of years of knowing and information.

As we run the Earth energy coming through the femur head, it enlivens our bone marrow and transfers the electrons into our blood. The energy flows through, spreads out through the butterfly bone of the pelvis, and then it returns to the Earth in continuous flow, a continuous circuit down the grounding corridor to our still point in the flow of mantle.

So much is involved in our connecting to Earth iron energy from a structural standpoint in the body. Earth iron energy, because it flows in the bone marrow, must communicate through the spaces of the ankles, the knees, and hips. Due to their movements and functions, these spaces aid us in healing our tendons in those three joints, in addition to being associated with the human position.

Practice Segment 07 – Earth Iron Energy Flow

Seated Practice coming into Position

Sit supported relaxed in your chair, legs at a right angle, hips and knees straight with your hip bones. Arms relaxed on your lap, your hands up. Place your shoulders where they feel most relaxed. Rest your head in a neutral position.

Center of the Head Practice

Exhale.
Pause. Connect thumb to pinky finger, be with soul essence sphere in center of head.
Inhale. Soul essence sphere in the center of your head pulses out to meet.
Exhale.
Inhale. Soul essence sphere continues to expand out till it reaches the size of a large marble.
Exhale. Soul essence sphere pulses in like a heartbeat.
Inhale. Soul essence sphere pulses out to meet.
Exhale. Soul essence sphere pulses in gathering its soul essence energy.
Inhale. Soul essence sphere pulses out to meet.
Continue soul essence pulse breath as long as you feel you need to, in order to connect to your soul essence pulse in the aural or physical center of your head.

With Soul Essence

Exhale.
Pause. On the pause of the exhale, connect thumb to pinky.
Inhale when you are ready.

Exhale.

Pause. On the pause of the exhale, connect thumb to pinky. In that pause, be with your soul essence pulse in the aural center or physical center of head.

Inhale when needed.

Regular breath. Continue and be with your soul essence sphere.

Exhale. On the pause of the exhale, connect thumb to pinky. Be with your soul essence sphere.

Inhale. Soul essence sphere in the aural or physical center of your head pulsates out to size of a large marble.

Exhale. On the pause of the exhale, connect thumb to pinky. Still in the pause, greet the soul essence sphere in the aural or physical center of your head.

Inhale when you need to. As you inhale, continue to allow your soul essence sphere to expand to the size of a large marble.

Exhale. Allow your soul essence sphere to slowly pulsate in like a heartbeat. Pause, connect thumb to pinky, and be with your soul essence sphere in the aural center of your head. Imagine snuggling into this safe space in the aural or physical center of your head.

Inhale when you need to, soul essence sphere pulsates like a heartbeat out to meet.

Repeat this for two to three breaths. Allow yourself to be nurtured by your soul essence.

Grounding

Exhale.

Pause. In the pause of the exhale, greet your four aspects of grounding. First greet the aspect of the feminine on the left side.

Regular breath.   Greet the aspect of the feminine. Be aware if it is in communication or out of communication and ask, through the center of your head and from your soul essence sphere, for it to be in communication.

Exhale.   In the pause of the exhale, greet the grounding aspect of the masculine on the right side of your grounding disc. Ask for it to be in communication.

Regular breath.

Exhale.

Pause. In the pause of the exhale, greet the aspect of the finite, which is the back position of the grounding disk, and ask it to be in relationship.

Regular breath.

Inhale.

Exhale. In the pause of the exhale, greet the aspect of the infinite, which is the front position of the grounding disk, asking it to be in relationship.

Regular breath.

Inhale.

Exhale.

Grounding corridor pulsates downward, in communication with your still point in the flow of mantle.

Aural Opening

Inhale. As we inhale, breathe into the sternum, opening.

Exhale. Let the sternum relax down and a little bit back.

Inhale. Sternum opening.

Exhale. Sternum relaxes down and back.

Continue these focused sternum breaths for three to four minutes or until you feel contained in your own electromagnetic field of your heart.

Earth Iron Energy Flow

Regular Breath.

As we contain our energy and we connect with our soul essence in physical form, our body builds the energy it needs to begin to open up its vortexes to outside flow. One of the energies that we use for transformation is Earth iron energy - it aids our communication and ultimately charges energy in our blood.

From the aural or physical center of head, greet each foot vortex.

In the center of your instep on the bottom of your foot, directly in front of your heal pad, there is a vortex (one on each foot).

From the aural center of your head or physical center of head, ask for your feet vortexes to open to a comfortable flow. They will slightly pulse down and, as they pulse down, they stop communicating with your energetic field and start communicating with the energetic field of Earth.

In this communication, we open up to the energy transfer, two fields meeting. The flow of Earth iron energy comes in each foot vortex, flowing into the foot, nurturing and healing the foot, flowing up and in, following the bone of the ankle and into the space of the ankle. We communicate through the space of the ankle into the bones, the tibia and fibula of the calves, communicating through the knee, into the bone marrow of the femurs, communicating through the femur heads, into the butterfly bone of the pelvis, moving across the butterfly bone of the pelvis and down the grounding. Allow continuous Earth iron flow.

Stay with this for two to five minutes.

Release feelings or heaviness and let micro-adjustments or micro shifts in the body occur.

Keep your relationship embodied feet vortexes adjusted to a comfortable flow.

Be with your soul essence in the aural center of your head or physical center of head.

Continue to allow your grounding aspects to talk - the feminine to the masculine, the masculine to the finite, and the finite to the infinite.

Exhale.

Pause. In the pause of the exhale, connect thumb to pinky finger.

Inhale. Move your thumb to put pressure on your ring finger. Allow your soul essence pulse, like a heartbeat, to slightly pulsate out.

Pause. In the pause of the breath, connect thumb to middle finger. Allow your soul essence sphere in the center of your aural head or physical center of head to pulse and meet.

Exhale. Connect thumb to pointer. Allow the soul essence sphere in the aural center of your head or physical center of head to pulsate in, like a heartbeat.

Pause. In the pause of the exhale, be with your soul essence sphere and know the energy gathers, as you run Earth iron energy in the bone marrow of your legs and pelvis, you are in communication with the information contained in the iron of Earth.

Repeat this for two to three minutes or until you settle into it.

Closing of Earth Iron Flow

Exhale.
Pause. In the pause of the exhale, through your soul essence sphere, ask your feet vortexes to slowly close. Earth iron flow slowly comes to a stop.
Inhale.

Close Practice

Exhale. From your soul essence in the center, or aural center of the head, allow your soul essence sphere to begin contracting into the size of a grain of sand or a seed, whichever is more comfortable for you while not in active Embodied Practice.
Inhale. Inhale when you are ready.
Exhale. Soul essence contracts in. The sphere grows denser, but loses no soul essence as it contracts in.
Inhale. Inhale when you are ready.
Exhale. Soul essence contracts in.
Continue your soul essence pulsation, with or without connecting thumb to pinky, as you read these words. Take as many exhales as you need until your sphere is the size of a grain of sand or a seed. Contracting the sphere down to the size of a grain of sand or seed, we lose no soul essence energy, but we draw less of this unwanted attention. This protects what is precious and only ours.
Regular breath.

Balancing out Your Energy

Balance out any excess energy that may have built up during practice in the following way:
Relax all the muscles of the neck, allowing the head to droop down, nose pointing toward the floor
Release the arms and hands so they also droop toward the floor.
One vertebra at a time, starting from the top one, nearest the neck, release the vertebra as you bend the spine slowly down, hands moving toward the floor.
Open the palms up, facing the floor for most, or for some with the flexibility, the palms will touch the floor. Release any excess energy that may have built up during practice.
Imagine a pulley between your shoulder blades, and when you are ready, imagine it pulling you up, one vertebra at a time, starting from the one closest to the tailbone.
Stack one vertebra on top of the other, as the pulley moves you slowly to an upright position.
Lastly, allow your neck to rest comfortably on the atlas, the top bone of the spine.

Chapter 9

Sky Flow

Embodied Sky Flow

Those of us that have been experientially reading this book by activating and using the parts of the Healing Practice are in the midst of an amazing metamorphosis, given the fact that the Practice is actual mechanisms of energy and photon light transfers, not visualizations. As we claim our space in the body and our soul essence sphere in the center of our heads, some of us may experience great joy, sorrow or both since our essence is returning to its rightful position in communication with the body. Some of us may need to practice the aural center of head if you are feeling headachy as your body adjusts to the energy.

As you charge your aura and use the Breath of Life, you meet people with an awareness of your contained energy and with a field that can interface with theirs instead of becoming, or being vulnerable to, the affects of others' energy. Dreams are also most likely changing. As you communicate with the flow of Earth iron energy the world may appear very different. Welcome to the beginning stages of Embodiment.

Opening to What Is Above: Sky Energy

First we learn to walk then we learn to run. With Embodied Practice, we learn to communicate with the four layers of Earth's atmosphere, that tell us to come into relationship first with the container we live in. The atmosphere of Earth is one of the mechanisms that communicate with the Sky energy or the energies of the solar system and Universe.

Think about being human here on Earth, and about the wanting or longing to communicate with something that has information that will support us in our life. We have learned that Earth energy supports us in being here on Earth's journey. Sky energy also has the information that supports our being here on Earth.

Let us suppose I am flown to Mars and when I get to Mars I don't know what to do, what to follow, what mechanisms are available, or how to behave. Someone tells me it is possible to connect to the cosmic energy with that star over there. They tell me to connect to the energy and the star's energy will give me information about life. So, I connect to the energy from that star and it tells me many things, many fascinating wonderful things. However, I wouldn't really have a mechanism for knowing what that would mean for my new experience on Mars or what I should be doing on Mars. I might interpret the many things differently. I may show up at things in certain ways that might not be appropriate or be left with a deep desire to figure things out. Because I get information from a distant star, not information from Mars, I miss the true experience of life on Mars.

Our human longing to figure things out (when we are not in communication with where we are) is most intense. When our longing is most great, we come up with the complicated theories or mechanisms to make ourselves believe we can find our way within the abyss.

Sky energy is literally the four layers of Earth's atmosphere. First, we come into relationship with the atmosphere because it tells us about being here on Earth (we have to know where we are before we can proceed). Secondly, our connection with Sky energy is the mechanism of communicating to the cosmic sea. Our connection to Sky flow develops the language center of our brain to be able to clearly understand the cosmic energy. Without the language of Sky energy, we perceive illusion as reality and we have to make stuff up to stay sane.

Layers of Sky

So we can awaken to what is, let's discuss the layers of the atmosphere - scientifically. The first layer of our atmosphere, called the troposphere, is where we live and where all our weather occurs. This is also where the winds are. The winds are very effective at keeping a very healthy mix of healthy air. For example, the rain forest produces much of the planet's oxygen that we breathe. All four of the directional winds help spread that oxygen through the entire atmosphere. Thus, the winds help keep a good healthy mix of what is in the air.

From an energetic standpoint, most of us can relate - because we have all been outside on a day where there is a very strong northern or southern wind. In this experience we know and can sense the differences of what the winds are bringing and what they do to us just by having that wind blow by us. The southern wind is a very warm and nurturing wind. An eastern wind is very refreshing and very movable. It is renewing and allows us to have permission within our being. The north wind is the quickening wind. It is an initiating wind. It motivates and gives us information on how to initiate things. The western wind is often a warm wet wind. It supports us in moving inward or moving toward inner growth. Those are the basic meanings of what could easily become a novel or manuscript - focusing on just the winds, on how we communicate with them, and on how we would use them in our life. We will learn a simple way to communicate with the four winds in activating the mechanisms with energy in human form in our body through connecting to Sky energy through our body.

The next layer of the atmosphere is the stratosphere. The lower layer of the stratosphere is where airplanes fly for most of their trip. There is not much turbulence in the lower end of the stratosphere because most of the winds occur in the troposphere. But in the higher reaches of the stratosphere, a very magical thing happens - this is where oxygen absorbs the ultraviolet rays, called the Ultraviolet Sea. Some ultraviolet rays get through down to Earth, the ones that are not too harmful to us. The very harmful ultraviolet rays get absorbed by the oxygen in the stratosphere. When the ultraviolet rays are absorbed by the oxygen, it splits the oxygen molecule (O_2) into single oxygen atoms (O), whereupon these oxygen atoms combine with oxygen molecules to form O_3 which is ozone.

Then the O_3 gets hit by ultraviolet radiation changing it back to O_2. This is a wondrous self-sustaining process of how transformation back and forth protects us.

Look at this from the different standpoint of the sun being the center of our solar system. The gravity of the sun allowed us to form, creating this space in which we are. The sun, on an energetic level, has much to tell and share with us. The fact that in this layer of the atmosphere, this very wondrous process is occurring; absorbing of some of the ultraviolet energy from the sun as it comes into our atmosphere. On this level, the stratosphere holds much information. Very potent communication can come from this layer of Sky. It is also important to note that the ozone layer and creation process is a self-sustaining one.

The third layer of Sky energy is the mesosphere. This layer of the atmosphere is where most of the meteorites find their way. Whether they are a few inches in diameter, a little bigger, or huge, most of these meteorites don't get through to Earth because of the protective mesosphere. For the survival of our planet, this layer is a very important part of our atmosphere. From an energetic standpoint, the layer is important in activating our ability to communicate with these parts of the atmosphere. This part of the atmosphere is very rich in information. It holds information that has traveled on the minerals, such as water in some of the meteorites that have come and have burned up in this layer of the atmosphere. Think of an atomic bomb explosion where objects and people left residual images behind on rocks or walls. This happens on a very similar layer on the mesosphere. In this layer, we are able to access much information to awaken to the mechanisms of Sky flow energy within our system and then, over time, when our vortexes learn to be in communication with the information and learn its language.

The last layer of Sky is the thermosphere. This is the uppermost layer, above the atmosphere and is extremely hot. During the day it can reach up to 4,500 degrees Fahrenheit (but a thermometer would read below 0 – it is near vacuum and heat loss far exceeds heat imparted by the sparse molecules there). It is in this part of Earth's electromagnetic field, its outside edge, where vortexes open and close to the sun. This is also the area where Auroras appear. It is a magic of beautiful images of light and color, which also have a vibration and a frequency (all lights and colors have a frequency) and thus have something to communicate.

That concludes our scientific understanding of the atmosphere, with a little understanding of what Sky energy is, from an energetic standpoint. Remember, each layer has something to communicate to us. Imagine our person on Mars, connecting only to the one star they were told to connect to, and in doing so, missing the existence of all of the information each layer of the atmosphere has to communicate to them. How would they get out of the abyss?

The mechanism for opening up to Sky energy is what, in Embodied Practice, we call our Embodied Relationship Halo Vortex. This vortex is located at the top of our head and is our 7th Vortex. Ancient people called it the crown chakra. When it is open, it looks and acts more like a halo. In the interest of being specific and honoring what is seen and known we call it the Halo Vortex.

The Halo Vortex is the seventh main vortex in the body; it may be easier to think of it this way and it is probably familiar to some of you. When we begin to open the seventh up, we first pulse open much like a whirlpool pulsing open. In the 7th Vortex, energy would spike up a little off the body giving it the halo look. This is the energetic mechanism of beginning to connect with what is above. It is the first mechanism that we will use to open to Sky flow.

When we open the 7th Vortex we bring in Sky energy, which includes the four winds energy, the amazing absorption process of the UV rays, the meteor information, and the light information from all of the layers that surround the Earth. This energy comes in and we start with having just a little bit of Sky energy at a time, so we don't hurt ourselves. When we invite a little bit of it in, the energy comes in through the top of our head and then arcs back following the path of the skull bone on the outside line of the bone. We never run Sky energy in the actual bone. It follows the arcs of the bone, arching down the back of the skull bone to our atlas. At our atlas, which is the top bone of our spine at the top of your neck, the energy divides into two thin lines and flows down the back in between the muscle structures along both sides of the spine.

If you look at a picture without the long muscles of the back, you will notice little lace muscles that look like stitching or sewing. These muscles are laced in and around every vertebrae, holding the integrity of the movement of the vertebrae. When people get an intense back pain it usually begins with one of these fine little lacey tendons getting a huge contraction, which causes all the other muscles to contract. The Sky energy runs above these little lace muscles, below the big long muscles of the back, through the space in between those muscle structures.

The Sky energy streams down the muscles of your spine and into your sacrum, the five fused vertebrae at the bottom of your spine. It moves through the top of our sacrum, below our 2nd Vortex, and above our 1st Vortex. It flows through the middle of the body on its way to the front and runs upwards through the long muscles of the abdomen to the sternum. Then it follows the path of the sternum and at the collarbone it separates again and goes out to each collarbone. Again it doesn't go into the collarbone, but simply follows the line. It communicates through the shoulder and follows the line of the upper arm. It communicates through the elbow, following the line of the main bone and forearm, and communicates through the wrist and out through the hand vortexes. Our hand vortexes are located in the fatty part of the palm below the thumb and right in between the middle finger and ring finger. This is the path of Sky energy that flows when we open in Embodied Practice.

Sky Flow Energy (Four layers of Earth's atmosphere)

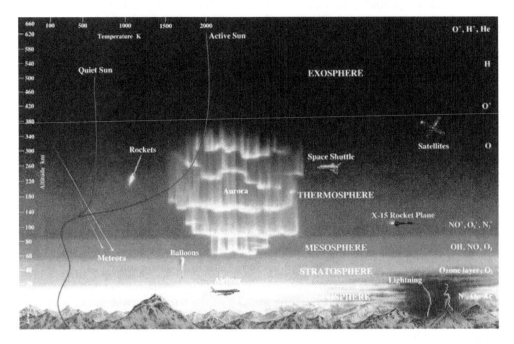

Before we continue, let us review our Four-Part Breath. For those of you that are practicing your Four-Part Breath, you may be up to maybe three or four seconds for each aspect of the breath. Or, if you have been practicing it every day, maybe you are able to hold up to five to six seconds for each aspect of your breath. Let's now practice a few settling breaths to help our body remember Sky, our container from which we emerged.

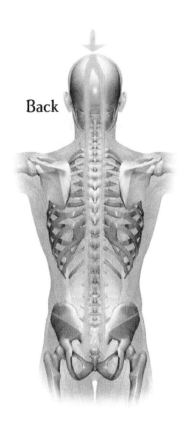

Back

Practice Segment 08 - Sky Flow

Seated Practice coming into Position

Sit supported, relaxed in your chair, legs at a right angle, hips and knees in alignment with your hip bones, arms relaxed on your lap, your hands up. Place your shoulders where they feel most relaxed. Rest your head in a neutral position.

Center of the Head Practice

Exhale.
Pause. Connect thumb to pinky finger. Be with soul essence sphere in aural or physical center of head.
Inhale. Soul essence sphere in the aural or physical center of your head pulses out to meet.
Exhale.
Inhale. Soul essence sphere continues to expand out till it reaches the size of a large marble.
Exhale. Soul essence sphere pulses in like a heartbeat.
Inhale. Soul essence sphere pulses out to meet.
Exhale. Soul essence sphere pulses in gathering its soul essence energy.
Inhale. Soul essence sphere pulses out to meet.
Continue soul essence pulse breath as long as you feel you need to, to connect to your soul essence pulse in the aural or physical center of your head.

(Note: This is a powerful soul self-position practice that can be used in any life circumstance to gain functional support of ourselves.)

With Soul Essence

Exhale.

Pause. In the pause of the exhale, connect thumb to pinky.

Inhale, when you are ready.

Exhale. In the pause of the exhale, connect thumb to pinky. In that pause, be with your soul essence pulse in the aural or physical center of head. Inhale when needed.

Regular breath. Continue and be with your soul essence sphere.

Exhale.

Pause. In the pause of the exhale, connect thumb to pinky. Be with your soul essence sphere.

Inhale. Soul essence sphere in the aural or physical center of your head pulsates out to size of a large marble.

Exhale.

Pause. In the pause of the exhale, connect thumb to pinky. Still in the pause, greet the soul essence sphere in the aural or physical center of your head.

Inhale. Continue to allow your soul essence sphere to expand to the size of a large marble.

Exhale. Allow your soul essence sphere to slowly pulsate in like a heartbeat.

Pause. Connect thumb to pinky finger. Be with your soul essence sphere in the aural or physical center of your head. Imagine snuggling into this safe space in the aural center of your head.

Inhale, when you need to. Soul essence sphere pulsates like a heartbeat out to meet. Repeat this for two to three breaths. Allow yourself to be nurtured by your soul essence.

Four-Part Breath

Exhale.

Pause. On the pause of the exhale, connect your thumb to your pinky, allowing your body to begin to settle into the practice.

Inhale. Connect thumb to ring finger.

Pause. Connect thumb to middle finger, holding in the fullness of breath.

Exhale. Connect thumb to pointer finger.

Pause. In the pause, connect thumb to pinky, settling.

Inhale. Connect thumb to ring finger.

Pause. In the fullness of breath, connect thumb to middle finger.

Exhale. Connect thumb to pointer.

Come around to that pause of the exhale.

(Do the Four-Part Breath for two to three minutes)

Grounding

Exhale.

Pause. In the pause of the exhale, greet your four aspects of grounding. First greet the aspect of the feminine on the left side.

Regular breath. As you greet the aspect of the feminine, be aware if it is in communication or out of communication. Ask (through the aural or physical center of your head, your soul essence sphere) for it to be in communication.

Exhale.

Pause. In the pause of the exhale, greet the grounding aspect of the masculine on the right side of your grounding disc. Ask for it to be in communication.

Regular breath.

Exhale.

Pause. In the pause of the exhale, greet the aspect of the finite, which is the back position of the grounding disc, asking it to be in relationship.

Regular breath.

Exhale.

Pause. In the pause of the exhale, greet the aspect of the infinite which is the front position of the grounding disc, asking it to be in relationship.

Inhale.

Exhale.

Grounding corridor pulsates downward in communication with your still point in the flow of mantle

Earth Flow

Exhale.

Inhale. Soul essence pulse pulsates out like a heartbeat and Earth flow pulses on the outside of your grounding corridor up to charge the perineum.

Exhale.

Pause. In the pause of the exhale, through your soul essence sphere, greet your feet vortexes and ask them to pulse open to just the right level for Earth iron flow into your bone marrow. Earth iron flow, taught from our last class, comes in through the feet vortexes and communicates through the ankles, flowing into the tibia and fibula, and communicating through the knee into the bone marrow of the femur, communicating through the femur head, fanning out through the bone marrow of the butterfly bone of the pelvis and continues to flow down your grounding corridor. Allow your body to make micro shifts in your seated practice while you work with running this energy, being in communication and being grounded to your still point in the flow of mantle.

The practice is supported by letting the body make its micro shifts in the body.

Stay with the soul essence sphere in the center of your head, grounded through the four aspects of grounding, the feminine, the masculine, the finite and the infinite, supported by Earth iron energy running in our bone marrow, communicating through our red bone marrow, femur head and our butterfly bone of our pelvis.

Breath of Life Charging

Exhale.

Inhale. Connect thumb to ring finger, charging Breath of Life in the middle of our sacrum.

Exhale.

Inhale. Put pressure on thumb to ring finger, allow the charging the Breath of Life in the sacrum. Allow that energy to swirl inward on the left side and outward on the right side bringing that energy down charging the Breath of Life. When it is charged enough it will stream out and surround the outside edge of your aura field.

Sky Flow

Gold Clearing

Put your finger on the middle of your skull on the top of your head and push it very gently and turn it inward a few spirals and then outward a few spirals. This will awaken your physical halo, Embodied Relationship Halo Vortex.

Exhale.

Pause. In the pause of the exhale, from your soul essence sphere, ask for a dot of gold clearing energy to come to your Halo Vortex, and ask for it to clear out anything that has been programmed that would need to be in communication with a specific energy. If your Halo Vortex has been closed off to the four layers that house the information - ask for the Sky information that is about being on Earth.

Inhale. Gold energy pulsates out to the size of a pearl, clearing.

Exhale. Gold energy pulsates down to the size of a dot.

Continue to allow the gold pulse to clear and, when you are ready, that gold energy will just dissipate.

If you feel it needs to be done again, you can wait and, on the next pause of your exhale, you can invite another dot of gold clearing energy.

Repeat this three to four times if needed.

Interfacing with Sky Energy

Exhale.

Pause. On the pause of the exhale, connect thumb to pinky. Greet your Halo Vortex, your 7th Vortex, and ask it to open up just enough to meet with Sky energy and to begin to come into relationship.

Regular breath.

Take as much time with this first meeting as you need. You don't have to come and follow for long. Running Sky energy through our entire system, you can simply be here and take as many breaths as you want. Know that your Halo Vortex is pulsating up and interfacing with Sky energy, and is in communication at this point. Allow yourself to remember the relationship between Earth and Sky as your Halo Vortex reaches out and meets Sky.

Inhale.

Regular Breath.

The flow will begin to come in and arc back immediately along the skull bone. Flowing down, it will break off into two lines in between your rotatores longus and rotatores brevis muscles of the spine and the long muscles of your back spinalis. If it feels difficult, release any difficulty in your body. As the Sky energy runs down in between those muscle structures, allow the Sky energy to begin to flow. Release down your grounding and allow your body to micro shift. At first, it may only go down a little bit that is fine too. If you are not ready to move on and allow Sky flow to continue down your back, just be with your soul essence pulse in the aural or physical center of your head and do pulse breath. When it reaches the sacrum, it will arch through at the top of the sacrum, moving through the body. When you are ready, it will flow up the front. Many people experience different things at this point. Let your experience be as much as possible in meeting Sky energy. Whatever you are feeling in your body, I guarantee you someone else has experienced it and it's alright. Release down your grounding. You can just be with your soul essence pulse in the aural or physical center of your head. As the Sky energy reaches your sternum allow it to flow along the top of the sternum.

Exhale.

Allow your soul essence pulse to greet the channels along your collarbone leading to your arm channels. Allow the Sky flow to move up along the line of the collarbone, communicating through (as Earth energy does) the joints, through the shoulders, following the line of the humerus in the upper arm, communicating through the elbow, following the bones of the forearm (radius and ulna), communicating through the wrist and out the hands. Allow continuous Sky flow.

Regular Breath.

With your soul essence pulse supported between Earth and Sky, allow continuous Sky flow, supported by continuous Earth iron flow, grounded and in communication with the still space and with the flow of mantel. As the Sky energy flows through your back channels and up your front channels and down your arm channels, allow the flow to begin to heal the channel and continue to release anything uncomfortable down your grounding corridor.

Greeting the South Wind

Be in your regular breath pattern in your Embodied Practice and read the words. Let them flow through and into you. Sky energy contains a vast array of energy information. In the beginning we take in and learn to listen to the four winds.

Exhale.

Pause. In the pause of the exhale, greet the south wind.

Inhale.

Exhale.

Pause. In the pause of the exhale, know the south wind.

Inhale. The south wind contains the energy information that nurtures us.

Exhale. Allow, through Sky flow, the south wind to nurture the body.

Inhale. Release down your grounding any uncomfortable feelings.

Regular breath.

Be with your soul essence pulse while receiving from the south wind.

Greeting the East Wind

Exhale.

Pause. In the pause of the exhale, greet the east wind.

Inhale.

Exhale.

Pause. In the pause of the exhale, know the east wind.

Inhale. Know the east wind's refreshing, renewing energy.

Exhale. Allow the east wind to renew your body.

Inhale. Release downward, through your grounding, any stale energy in the body.

Regular breath.

Be with your soul essence pulse as you take in the renewing energy of the east wind.

Note: For some this may be enough for today. Go to the Close Practice Section below. Complete north and west winds at another practice session.

Greeting the North Wind

Exhale.
Pause. In the pause of the exhale, greet the north wind.
Inhale.
Exhale.
Pause. In the pause of the exhale, know the north wind.
Inhale. Hold the quickening, the ability to transfer energy from one thing to another connected to the stratosphere.
Regular breath.
Be with your soul essence pulse as you take in the quickening energy of the north wind.

Greeting the West Wind

Exhale.
Pause. In the pause of the exhale, greet the west wind.
Inhale.
Exhale.
Pause. In the pause of the exhale, know the west wind.
Inhale. Be with the information that comes on solar radiation, too toxic for it to reach us down through the layers of atmosphere, yet the west wind brings us information from the sun.
Regular breath.
Be with your soul essence pulse as you take in the information of the west winds.

Take as much time as is comfortable, supported between Earth and Sky, in your Embodied Practice. Be with the four winds.

Close Practice

Exhale. From your soul essence in the aural or physical center of the head, allow your soul essence sphere to begin contracting into the size of a grain of sand or a seed, whichever is more comfortable for you while not in active Embodied Practice.
Inhale. Inhale when you are ready.
Exhale. Soul essence contracts in. The sphere grows denser, but loses no soul essence as it contracts in.
Inhale. Inhale when you are ready.
Exhale. Soul essence contracts in.
Continue your soul essence pulsation, with or without connecting thumb to pinky, as you read these words. Take as many exhales as you need until your sphere is the size of a grain of sand or a seed. We contract the soul essence sphere to a smaller size. Contracting the sphere down to the size of a grain of sand or seed, we lose no soul essence energy.

Balancing out Your Energy

Balance out any excess energy that may have built up during practice in the following way:

Relax all the muscles of the neck, allowing the head to droop down, nose pointing toward the floor.

Release the arms and hands so they also droop toward the floor.

One vertebra at a time, starting from the top one nearest the neck, release the vertebra as you bend the spine slowly down, hands moving toward the floor.

Open the palms up, facing the floor for most or, for some with the flexibility, the palms will touch the floor. Release any excess energy that may have built up during practice.

Imagine a pulley between your shoulder blades, and when you are ready, imagine it pulling you up, one vertebra at a time, starting from the one closest to the tailbone.

Stack one vertebra on top of the other, as the pulley moves you slowly to an upright position.

Lastly, allow your neck to rest comfortably on the atlas, the top bone of the spine.

Focus Work

I would suggest you pick one focus, maybe one of the particular winds or one of the layers of the atmosphere, because each one holds very different information. Go into your practice and get supported, get grounded, and be with your soul essence pulse. Open up your Halo Vortex, your 7th vortex, to Sky energy flow and focus on knowing what a particular wind or layer of the atmosphere has for you today. Also, continue to practice your Four-Part Breath, and clear your healing to the thalamus and hypothalamic-pituitary-axis on the third ventricle, which is always our goal to heal.

Pulse Life Force Charging

Exhale. Soul essence sphere pulses in gathering energy, Earth energy pulses up the outside line of the grounding corridor, charging the perineum - this charges the vortex core.

Inhale. Soul essence sphere pulsates out to meet and our life force energy pulses down the inside of the grounding corridor to meet Earth.

Do this for seven to twenty breaths.

Chapter 10

Human Vortexes

Introduction

Calling of Vortexes

Moving into reflective relationship requires seeing the human energy centers in the body as they function in relationship so they communicate with the pulse fields of the Universe. This moved me to call these human energy centers a name that represents their function. In the past, these energy centers have been called many different names. A name that limits function limits our ability to see it for what it is. In order to be free to see clearly and emerge into a soul orientated connection to everything, we need to release the old names of the energy centers in the body. If the old names are not released, the names pull our prefrontal lobe into a locked position and all information about the human energy centers is limited, based upon what has historically been associated with them.

Mirroring Vortex of Earth

In Embodied Practice, we hold a different knowing about how energy centers in the body develop and what their functions are. I am setting them free by giving them a general name based on their form, vortexes. This name opens us to a greater understanding of their developed process, function and of how they are the key of our energetic existence.

In Embodied Practice, we see energy centers in the body first as mirrors of the space-time vortex created by Earth's sitting in the vibration strands of space. In Einstein's Theory of Relativity this is called the space-time vortex. As Earth formed and gathered her mass, she took her orbit around the sun and created the space-time vortex. This chapter will awaken you to what your mirrored connection to the space-time vortex means.

Our vortexes, in their basic form or shape, mirror the form and shape of the space-time vortex of Earth. Our vortexes follow the four-layered pattern of the space-time vortex. Mirroring through our creation is a complex mechanism revealing the levels of inner connection. A basic example of this mirroring is seen in how trees and plants grow - the fractal pattern of the upper tree or plant is mirrored in the root pattern. When the root system of a tree is too compromised, the tree dies. It can no longer be in its mirrored relationship to Earth without its mirrored fractal pattern.

In the above example and in energetic life, when a mirrored aspect of creation is distorted, the mirrored disturbance creates devolution. Knowing this aids us in awakening to what occurred when the ancient form of understanding of energy centers called "chakras" had an outward pulsation, a horizontal (not a vertical) position cannot mirror Earth's space-time vortex. This horizontal meeting of vortexes puts humans and Earth off phase. This shift in the vortexes was so widespread among the human race that our ability to communicate and connect through time and space was lost. Connecting to the concept of mirroring human vortexes to Earth's space-time vortex awakens us to how humans have lost their potential. There is a natural process that humans follow to develop their vortexes to stay in communication. Since the level of development in each vortex is mirrored from the parent's vortexes to their child's vortexes, over time our energetic centers lost the ability to connect. With each generation, we lost more and more of our basic functions and structures from which human evolution cascades. Eventually, the loss took us out of our vortexes and other structures that the soul essence can use to orient ourselves, to know where we are in the Universe.

Prior to the time that humanity lost vortex connection, mirroring the vortexes began in the uterus and during the first few months of life outside the womb. In the coming chapters, the basic structure and activations will be taught to reclaim our space-time connection which used to be. We will first orient and activate the basic form and flow of each vortex, which were first mirrored from our parents.

For some of you, this mirroring lends a new understanding of how we end up like our parents. Many people, even with decades of therapy and self-help work, still manifest (in some way) a behavior with the energetic patterns of one or more parent even though they try desperately to not be like their parents. When the vortexes form fully, we are not like them because we mirror our human place in evolution and are in relationship through our soul essence.

Embodied Awakening

I am honored and grateful for this opportunity to explain my Embodied Awakening of the human energy centers in the body. Their shape and function mirror the four-dimensional vortex. Earth sits within the fabric of space and time, lining up with the electromagnetic polar vortexes, which are created at the north and south poles of Earth.

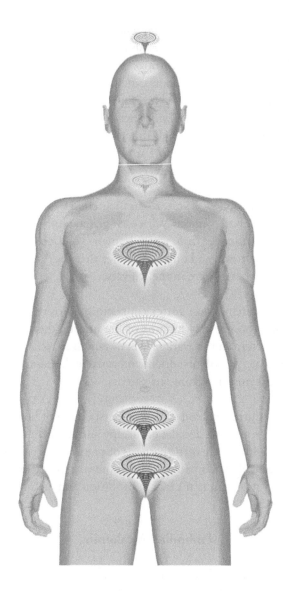

Unseen, Yet Seen

Einstein spoke of the space-time vortex Earth sits in and documented its existence in 1905. On May 4, 2011, the Gravity Probe charted the space-time vortex and shape matched it to the description from Einstein's Theory of Gravity. The shape was exactly what Einstein described it would be 106 years earlier. Einstein saw the unseen through mathematics in his brain.

We can take a very simple example that we all experienced many times in our lives. When we get sick with a virus or bacteria, we are not able to see this virus or bacteria. Yet we know in all certainty that we have it through the experience of our bodies. We go to a doctor, who in all certainty confirms we have it.

In today's age of testing, a doctor will not commit to a diagnosis until they do a swab test or maybe a blood test. The tests allow them to see the virus or bacteria and commit to a diagnosis. We don't usually need the swab test or the blood test, because we know we have a virus or bacteria based on the symptoms and affects of having either one. This swab test doesn't make the virus more real.

So, the shape and development of our human vortexes is in the unseen realm, yet each of us daily experience how the lack of development in our human vortexes keeps us out of pure experience. Our developed vortexes are the platform for having heaven on earth, free of the human field.

Our DNA turns on and off via vibrational signals. The loss of our vortex communication through time and space facilitates the devolution of our DNA because they no longer receive the ongoing vibratory signal they need to be healthy and evolve.

Developing Vortexes

Each of the vortexes is contained in the physical form in the body. They are nurtured by a system of flow in the body which is set up through life experience. Besides the mirroring from parents, which is the beginning of the forming of the vortex structure, the 13 Energetic Stages of Humans through development will fill in the rest of the basic structures of each vortex. Then through our lifetime, our soul essence fills in the rest. The 13 Energetic Stages of Humans will cover the vortex basics, their elements, aspects, basic abilities and their points of origin of vibratory communication. The flow systems in the body are completely related to the 13 Energetic Stages of Humans. Completion of these stages facilitates the forming of the four layers of the vortexes and how they function, how they communicate with our DNA, with our personality, and how they function with our abilities to communicate across time and space free of the human field.

To further awaken to knowing that we are energetic developmental beings, how our life experience develops the form and flow of each vortex, and how the form and flow of each vortex determines our character and experience of life, we will utilize the diagnosis of narcissism.

In my theory of Sensology, the point of origin of narcissism is when a child's true innocent love of the mother or father is used against them. In other words, our innocent love in the vortex is an energetic flow which would be contained and used to fuel our energetic lives. When the parent is in need of a child turning over their innocent love of the parent to fill a need of the parent, narcissism can result. This occurs across the stages from birth to around age six, when it is cemented in, because the 4th Vortex tips forward and can't tip back into its embodied position without the healing practice, over time.

In the fifth development stage of The Theory of Sensology, Seeds of Passion and Position, we complete three energetic tasks. One is containment. It is here where the 4th Vortex is establishing itself as a safe container of the soul essence, when it is time again to communicate with the soul essence. But when the developing child is forced by the actions of the parents to turn over their love, to some of their love, or to validate the parent, the vortex cannot contain and tips forward.

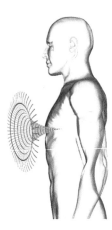

So this person in the field of psychology would be diagnosed with narcissism. This person will not be able to access his/her soul essence information or charge his/her own energy. When one cannot charge their own energy, they go looking for something outside themselves. Books on narcissism call this narcissism supply. They must get energy from other people.

> *"The separation understanding of the soul began with the monolithic belief systems. It will end with our acceptance that all there is, is emergence."*
> **- Kiera D. Laike IRW**

Essence of Soul

In all ways, humans mirror every aspect of creation – when our vortexes are developed and filled in with our crystal structures of our soul essence. This mirroring occurs through the connection to the 4x4 to Infinity (the pulse fields). No linear understanding or connection to who we are can connect us to the pulse fields. Today, our awakening to ourselves as souls has been brought into being when the Body-Mind-Spirit movement came from the human field. This splitting (the separation of body, mind, and spirit) keeps us in a war with our bodies and out of connection to the 4x4 to Infinity process of joy.

Our search or meeting of the soul, separate from the body or mind, only separates us more from being the reflection of the soul essence in physical form. Separating our mind or neural processes keeps it in linear process and the dark energy housed in our brains never develops or connects. Without oneness, we never develop or connect to be with the unseen energy and interconnections of the Universe.

To clarify, the soul is different than the soul essence. The soul essence is the connection of all, yet the least known or understood. Your soul essence is everywhere, yet nowhere. It is something that creates and goes in and out of physical being, yet holds the key and is the mechanism of coming into vibratory bioelectric being, through the containing of photon light in human form.

It is my perception that a lot of the confusion about the soul comes from false attachments to what will happen to the soul or what has happened to the soul. The soul essence, taking the journey of being embodied in human form, works to be in relationship through a pulse field in infinite ways via the human body. Practice sessions in the following chapters of each vortex briefly touch on a few ways the soul essence comes into relationship and how the soul is created through form, the core interconnecting column of each vortex.

I have been teaching the Embodied Principle of 4x4 to Infinity, called "Being Met", for a decade now, and I still struggle with how to teach infinity without attaching to it. My students struggle as well, yet the more we gather our soul essence, the more it perfectly is.

The meeting and splitting form the vortexes (partly).

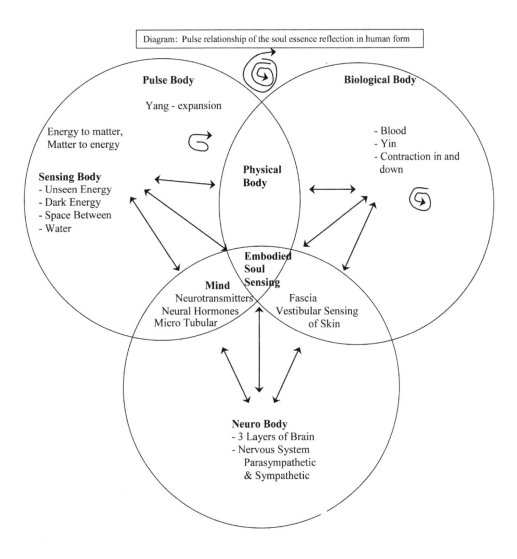

Diagram: Pulse relationship of the soul essence reflection in human form

The Arrows depict interactive relationships – all of which can fall under 4x4 to Infinity. Each of the interrelated spheres represents who are, when we develop the ability to be in connection at any point with all aspects of the 4x4 to Infinity.

It is my desire for this diagram to be the beginning of understanding the soul essence's complex reflection in human form. I longingly remind readers that this is NOT a diagram of the soul essence; it is a functional diagram of the soul that develops as part of the developing body becoming the vehicle for the essence to come into relationship through the human body.

This sets us free from the split that comes to the human consciousness every time we say, "body, mind, spirit." We treat each of them as separate parts whenever we say this. The soul is not a separate entity in the body because it *is* the body; the mind is the mirrored reflection of the body, soul essence, and vortexes development. The diagram does point out and lets us see that the essence through pulse relationship is at the core in everything.

In the diagram, the physical body is where the biological body and pulse body meet. The meeting of the pulse body and the neural body is the mind. The neural body and the biological body meet and are in relationship through the fascia. The embodied soul sensing is at the core of experience in the body.

> *"The soul, to be complete in each incarnation, must fully inhabit each part – like a flower dropped in water, each drop holds the reflection of the flower."*
>
> **- Kiera D. Laike, IRW**

Chapter 11

Embodied Form and Flow
The 1st Vortex

Embodied Relationship

As I awaken us to the reflective developmental nature of our human vortexes, a new name and definition continues to emerge. It is important to define the categories. There are two types of vortexes, Embodied and Embodied Relationship. The Embodied Vortexes are the 2nd, 3rd, 4th, 5th, and 6th Vortexes. There are two Embodied Relationship Vortexes, the 1st Vortex (Form and Flow Vortex) and the 7th Vortex (Halo Vortex). Embodied Relationship Vortexes are positioned both in and outside of the physical structure of the human body. In other words, these vortexes' daily functions dictate their occupying space, both inside and outside the human body. As with Embodied Vortexes, they occupy (for daily functions only) space inside the body. For special time-limited functions, Embodied Vortexes tip forward and briefly occupy a space both in and out of the body, some of which were discussed in Chapter 10.

Our 1st Vortex provides our communication with water. Without being in communication through water humans cannot form or flow. The 1st Vortex is located at the end of the spinal column nerves between the sacrum and coccyx. Nerve endings create a pulse field, designed to be in communication with water. In the uterus, it is also the 1st Vortex to form as the sperm enters the egg, calling the body into form through communication with water. In communication with water, our chromosomes line up and we energetically emerge into body from which the next soul forms. As humans, we develop in water. We breathe water and experience our first vibratory communications through water. This communication with water is the point of origin for humans bringing into form. The form brings us into pulse relationship with the electromagnetic energy inside and outside of us on planet Earth.

Aspect

Our original biological form on earth emerged from water. Communication with water sustains us on a biological level. Thus, the aspect of the 1st Vortex is biological process. Our epigenes (our DNA snips) turn on and off from our energetic experiences in the body. Without connections and communication with water, our health wanes and our epigenes down-regulate.

Abilities

Our 1st Vortex has a core set of abilities, as do all the vortexes. The core ability in the 1st Vortex is communication through water, connection to form and flow, and providing the base of our intuition beyond our cognitive ability to understand the world via our prefrontal lobe.

Each of the abilities is best learned or understood through experience. Each vortex chapter includes an activation practice that awakens the core ability of each vortex. These activations aid us in awakening to our mirrored relationship with the space-time vortex of Earth.

Note: To be clear, as we bring the Embodied Awakening to our human vortexes, "abilities" refers to the functions that each vortex performs when they form. If the vortexes are not formed, the person is without that ability.

Practice Segment 09 - Form and Flow Vortex

Aspect Clearing; Clear Blockage of Flow or Communication

In this chapter, we will learn to create and use a clearing vortex. This clearing vortex is one that is created in the electromagnetic field of Earth. It is a portal vortex that meets our Embodied Relationship Vortexes (on a field association level) to clear anything that has formed in our vortexes which does not belong in human development.

When Earth and Sky energy meet, a clearing vortex is formed. When this happens, Earth and Sky energy support us to come into a reflective relationship and energy that shouldn't be is removed. When the portal closes the unhealthy energy is no more. What was created in that person is now removed.

Open your Embodied Practice. Follow the Seated Practice, Soul Essence in Center of Head, Grounding, Aural, Four-Part Breath, Earth Flow, and Sky Flow from the Supplemental Chapter.

Through your soul essence pulse in the center of your head, create a clearing vortex on the outside edge of the cobalt blue line of your aura.
Exhale.
Pause. In the pause of the exhale, through your soul essence sphere, greet Earth and ask it to send a stream of energy upward, stopping 19 to 22 inches out in front of you, at nose height.
Inhale.
Exhale.
Pause. Through your soul essence sphere, greet Sky and ask Sky to drop down a thin strand of energy to meet a strand of Earth energy.
Regular breath. The two energies will meet and will form the clearing vortex.

From the center of your head, greet your 1st Vortex.
Through your soul essence, ask for whatever is blocking the flow in your 1st Vortex - whatever blocks communication, whatever information or associations with the 1st Vortex that blocks you from being in communication through your 1st Vortex.
Allow it to move out of your 1st Vortex, in between the sacrum and coccyx. Move it into the clearing vortex, releasing anything that is able (at this time) that is not supposed to be part of your 1st Vortex.

If you feel uncomfortable in the body while clearing, adjust your Sky or your Earth flow, adjust your Halo Vortex a little bit, opening or closing it. From the center of your head, ask for your feet vortexes to open and close.

When the vortex has completed its clearing for today, it will close. Energy is cleared and transformed.

Clear Fear of Change

Exhale.

Pause. In the pause of the exhale, connect thumb to pinky finger. Through your soul essence sphere, ask for a clearing vortex to form on the outside edge of your cobalt blue line outside of your aura.

Charge the Breath of Life, if you need to. Line and define the outside edge of your aura. Be grounded and in communication with your sacred space in the flow of mantle, release into the clearing vortex fear of change.

Regular breath. Take two to six breaths.

When complete, the clearing vortex will close, the fear energy will dissipate. (Note: you may still have fear of change which is normal, yet it has begun to change. You have at least cleared what was ready in this moment).

Clear Soul Self-Doubt

Exhale.

Pause. In the pause of the breath, connect thumb to pinky finger. Through your soul essence sphere in the center of your head, ask for a clearing vortex to form on the outside edge of your aura.

Inhale.

Exhale.

Pause. In the pause of the exhale, through your soul essence sphere, greet Earth and ask it to send a stream of energy upward, stopping 19 to 22 inches out in front of you, at nose height.

Inhale.

Exhale.

Pause. Through your soul essence sphere, greet Sky and ask Sky to drop a thin strand of energy downward to meet a strand of Earth energy.

Regular breath. The two energies will meet and will form the clearing vortex.

Release soul self-doubt. From the center of your head, ask for the clearing vortex to attract in soul self-doubt.

Regular breath. Take two to six breaths releasing and adjusting your practice as you release. When complete, the vortex will close and the energy will dissipate.

Clear Fear of Not Being Worthy

Exhale.

Pause. In the pause of the breath, connect thumb to pinky finger. Ask through your soul essence for a clearing vortex to form on the outside edge of your aura.

Inhale.

Exhale.

Pause. In the pause of the exhale, through your soul essence sphere, greet Earth and ask it to send a stream of energy upward, stopping 19 to 22 inches out in front of you, at nose height.

Inhale.

Exhale.

Pause. Through your soul essence sphere, greet Sky and ask Sky to drop a thin strand of energy downward to meet a strand of Earth energy.

Regular breath. The two energies will meet and will form the clearing vortex.

From the center of your head, ask for fear of not being worthy to return to communication with water through flow.

Regular breath, two to six times.

When complete, the clearing vortex will close and the energy will dissipate.

Be with your soul essence pulse in the center of your head and in communication with your still point in the flow of mantle, supported by Earth flow and Sky flow, awakened to the knowledge of flow relationship and the ability of your 1st Vortex.

Our 1st Vortex is the form and flow vortex, enabling us to be in continuous communication, our point of origin of functional oneness. Our oneness allows for all to be in relationship.

Exhale.

Pause. In the pause of the exhale, connect thumb to pinky finger. Be with the information about our 1st Vortex.

Inhale.

Exhale.

Pause. In the pause, be with the information regarding the 1st Vortex.

Regular breath. Repeat this two to three times.

Put in Communication with Soul Essence and Still Point

Quartz Crystal Seed

Exhale.

Pause. In the pause of the exhale, from your soul essence pulse in the center of your head, ask for a quartz crystal seed to be created on the outside edge of your aura.

Supported in your Embodied Practice, ask from the center of your head, for the words "form and flow" to appear above the quartz crystal seed.

When you are ready, ask from the center of your head for the words "form and flow" to drop into the crystal seed. As the words drop into the seed, ask for them to change to the vibration of form and flow that your soul essence is ready to work from.

The seed will change to pure energy vibration. Allow yourself to sense, see, or know that it is there. The form and flow vibration will move into your 1st Vortex when ready. Do not force it, it is ever emerging.

Charge Flow in 1st Vortex

Exhale.
Pause. In the pause of the exhale, connect thumb to pinky finger. Be with form and flow in your 1st Vortex.
Inhale. Charge form and flow in your 1st Vortex.
Pause. Hold in the fullness of breath. Be with form and flow in your 1st Vortex.
Exhale. Move and sense through form and flow.
Regular breath.
Repeat this Four-Part Breath as many times as feels right.

1st Vortex Greets Still Point in Flow of Mantle

Exhale.
Pause. In the pause of the exhale, allow your soul essence to greet your 1st Vortex.
Inhale.
Exhale.
Pause. In the pause of the exhale, allow your still point in the flow of mantle to greet your 1st Vortex. The 1st Vortex, the center of form and flow in the body, is in communication with all and held by your still point in the flow of mantle, so that your soul essence can communicate within physical soul form.

Close your practice by following Closing of Practice and Complete Sections in the Supplemental Chapter.

Embodied Color

Each vortex has a point of origin color, which along with the vortex aspect, provides the beginning framework for each vortex to form into its four-layered structure mirroring the space-time vortex Earth created as it formed within the space-time continuum.

Clarity of What Is

Color association is connected to a frequency and wavelength. Vortexes pulsate and vibrate with their primary color's frequency and wavelength for their communication and function. Please note that vortex color is not associated with the reflective nature of color but with the functions of frequency and wavelength associated with each color.

Embodied vortex color activations are what we call point of origin vibrations. Point of origin vibration follows the main function of each vortex. To understand this, one must release any attachment to the existence of a higher vibration, for this takes one out of relationship. Each color is a frequency and therefore has a corresponding wavelength. In Embodiment, one aspires to be in relationship through frequency and wavelength communications. This is one of the multitudes of mechanisms of functional oneness. All of the cells in the body are 'one,' yet if one goes out of communication with the DNA, cancer can result. In functional oneness, the vortexes are in communication through their color wavelength frequency activation with what they emerged in relationship to within the body and Universe. To clarify, each of our Embodied Vortexes utilize all wavelengths and frequencies (as they develop), depending on what complex function they are performing for the soul-body. Physical and mental health - and the formation of each vortex - are always dictated by the vortex communicating at the point of origin wavelength and frequency, which is associated with its point of origin color.

What Frequency?

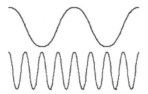

The color associated with each vortex provides the level of frequency and wavelength. The wavelength dictates the amount of space available for communication in each Embodied vortex.

A wave with a higher frequency has a shorter wavelength, dictating less space in between the waves. This allows the wavelength to penetrate more things and more things to penetrate it. An example is water, which we want to be in complete and full communication with. Think of loving someone so much yet you could never speak to them fully. Every time you had a conversation, you only heard a few words of all the thousands they told you. Over time, even though you loved them, you would lose an understanding of who they are. Over years or decades, you would go to get them something and it most likely would not be at all what they wanted. Each of us would not desire to find ourselves in such a relationship. Our point of origin vibration in the 1st Vortex, violet, allows us to hear all words of communication from water on planet Earth, so we can stay in relationship with Earth - giving us a complete conversation with the planet Earth.

In contrast, consider the level of communication that has occurred if we place a common color association with the 1st Vortex of the frequency of red. Red is a low frequency and therefore has long wavelengths. Long wavelengths limit communication, unlike shorter wavelengths that allow more communication. Thus, when we communicate with Earth, we only hear a few words of the thousands that Earth is telling us. We are out of relationship in time and space because our connection through water is one of the mechanisms of knowing our position in time and space.

Creating Change

Many of us long to create change on Earth. Change cannot be brought about when we are not in complete communication with the person or planet we wish to bring change to or on. The power of this and the truth of complete communication, being a mechanism of change, can be seen in a biological process called apoptosis (spontaneous cell death). This is what everyone with cancer hopes and prays will happen to their cancer.

When conditions are such in the body that the cancer cells are able to be put back into communication with the body's DNA, the cancer cells in a sense know they don't belong and kill themselves (apoptosis; spontaneous cell death). To rid ourselves of the cancer, humans have brought things into being, from being out of communication. We must be back in full communication to that which has been created on earth that harms us in order for apoptosis occur.

Color of the 1st Vortex

The point of origin color of the 1st Vortex is violet. Violet has a high frequency and short wavelength. This allows for complete and unblocked communication to Earth. It is critical to be in complete communication with wherever we are. Without this we can never live in flow and be.

In contrast, the poplar color for the 1st Vortex is red - which has low frequency and long wavelengths. This blocks communication with Earth, blocking us from our ability to be where we are. When communication with Earth was blocked, humans began to bring into form obsessions with spiritual focus that gave information about getting off the planet Earth. Sadly, human vortex and structure organization can only occur in the container of Earth in communication with water.

Practice Segment 10 - Color Activation of 1st Vortex

Note: Wait one to two weeks after vortex activation prior to doing color activation.

Open Embodied Practice by following the Seated Practice, Soul Essence in the Center of the Head, Grounding, Aural, Four-Part Breath, Earth Flow, and Sky Flow in the Supplemental Chapter.

Exhale.
Pause. In the pause of the exhale, connect thumb to pinky finger.
Through your soul essence pulse in the center of your head, create a clearing vortex on the outside edge of your aura.
Be with attracting what the vortex needs to clear (all vortexes are in relationship).
Inhale.
Exhale. From the center of your head, greet your 1st Vortex.
Through your soul essence, ask the clearing vortex to take out whatever blocks your 1st Vortex from containing the vibration and frequency of violet.
Inhale.
Pause.
Exhale.
Pause. In the pause of the exhale, continue to allow the clearing vortex to pull energy that is blocking the container of your 1st Vortex.
Note: Without the container and structure in functional form, the true vibration of the 1st Vortex will not take root.
The clearing vortex will close and the energy will dissipate when ready.

Note: If you feel uncomfortable during this clearing, remember to adjust your Earth and Sky flow, so that your body is supported in the practice. If you feel anxious, continue to use settling breath; on the pause of the exhale, connect thumb to pinky and release down your grounding corridor.

Regular breath.

Now that we have created the container to hold the functional aspect, which is vibration and frequency of full communication with water, strong feelings may come up that your vortex did not form in full communication when you were young.

Exhale.

Pause. In the pause of the exhale, ask a clearing vortex to form on the outside edge of your aura.

Take three to six Four-Part Breaths.

As we clear and do our Four-Part Breath, our feelings of being met begin to emerge. We are soul essence reflection developing in body. Our DNA, cell membranes, vestibular system, lymphatic system, and all other body systems long to be met. Feelings of warmth, security, contact and reflection emerge that the developing soul craves. It is this being met which allows the container of the 1st Vortex to form so it can hold the vibration of violet. If the developing *soul* is not met, it uses a protective measure - it deems that the place that it has been incarnated is not a safe place and so does not establish a communication with Earth. At this young point of life, the soul is not able to distinguish the difference between whether it is the human field that has become unsafe or the field of the Earth that has become unsafe.

Exhale. In the pause of the exhale, create a clearing vortex on the outside edge of your aura.

Begin to move any feelings that you have from your early childhood (one month to 18 months of age). Feelings could emerge from being fed wrong food, not given contact, etc. When you try to begin to establish your own container, you may experience deep grief (or deep sadness) from your mother not accepting your right to form your own container. Remember to stay in the center of your head as you allow the clearing vortex to absorb and draw those feelings of not being met.

When complete the vortex will close.

Violet Sphere

Exhale.

Pause. In the pause of the exhale, allow a violet sphere to form on the outside edge of your aura - the size of a drop of water.

Inhale.

Exhale.

Pause. In the pause of the exhale, connect thumb to pinky finger. Be with your soul essence in the center of your head. Be with the dot of violet on outside of your aura.

Inhale when ready, connect thumb to ring finger. Know the properties of being in communication, or taking in communication, through the vibration and frequency of violet.

Hold in the fullness of breath, thumb to middle finger. Allow communication with violet to be.

Exhale. Connect thumb to pointer finger. Be in relationship to the frequency of violet.

Repeat this Four-Part Breath 5 times.

Exhale. In the pause of the exhale, connect thumb to pinky. Through your soul essence pulse, greet the container in the core of your 1st Vortex.
Inhale. Pulsate down to meet the core of your 1st Vortex, connect thumb to ring finger.
Hold in the fullness of breath, connect thumb to middle finger. Be with the container in your 1st Vortex.
Exhale. On the exhale, connect thumb to pointer finger. Invite the violet energy to the exact center where the container formed, to accept the vibration and frequency of violet.
Regular breath for one to two minutes. Be with your soul essence sphere in the center of your head and with your 1st Vortex.

Exhale.
Pause. In the pause of the exhale, connect thumb to pinky finger. Think of one simple thing you would like to communicate with water about. It could be an aspect of your life. It could be an aspect of past, future, or anything that you would like to be in communication about. It could be something that you would like to tell or ask the water.
Inhale. Pulsate down to meet the core of your 1st Vortex, connect thumb to ring finger.
Hold in the fullness of breath middle finger. Be with the container in your 1st Vortex.
Exhale.
Pause. In the pause of the exhale, connect thumb to pointer finger. Be in communication with water and through violet frequency and vibration with whatever you would like to communicate about. Give yourself permission in the center of your head to know, sense, or see that the communication is occurring.
Regular breath. Take two to three minutes in communication with water.

Close your practice by following Closing of Practice and Complete Sections in the Supplemental Chapter.

Chapter 12

Embodied Sensing
The 2nd Vortex

The 2nd Embodied Vortex houses the element of Earth. Earth's soil is estimated to be 92-94% bacteria[1]. The 2nd Vortex pulse field is housed in and created by the life of the good bacteria in the large and small bowels. Bacteria are the point of origin of biological life on Earth and have so much to communicate to us through our 2nd Embodied Vortex and point of origin of sensing in the body.

Aspect

Sensing is the aspect of the 2nd Vortex. Sensing is critical in being human and being able to interpret those 5,000 signals coming at us in any given moment. Human tactile, visual, auditory, and olfactory senses, pick up anywhere from 100 to 300 incoming signals at a given moment. Our sensing systems, through our vortex development, are responsible for taking in the rest of the 4,700 to 4,900 incoming signals. Sensing is our super power in the Universe! Sensing, ultimately, is so complex that I cannot take it on in this book. Even my students who have been studying Embodied Practice with me for over a decade still marvel at the continuous connections through sensing. Briefly, sensing is a field-to-field transfer. Note that the Practice Segments in this book hold the point of origin to be your journey into sensing.

Abilities

For field-to-field transfer to occur, we must possess the ability to transfer energy and maintain our own field. The 2nd Vortex charges the body's chi or field energy point of origin. This is crucial and cannot be completed without energy from a population of good bacteria.

Practice Segment 11 - Activation of Sensing - The 2nd Vortex

Open your Embodied Practice by following the Seated Practice, Soul Essence in Center of Head, Grounding, Aural, Four-Part Breath, Earth Flow, and Sky Flow from the Supplemental Chapter.

Aspect Clearing of 2nd Vortex

From the center of your head, greet your 2nd Vortex. Your 2nd Vortex is located in your mid-lower abdomen, four to five fingers below your belly button.
Exhale. In the pause of the breath, connect thumb to pinky and in that moment of pause, be with your 2nd Vortex.

Allow your breath to continue. Inhale when you need to and, in every pause, be with your 2nd Vortex.

Clear Blockage of Flow or Communication

From the center of your head, create a clearing vortex on the outside edge of your aura. **Exhale.**

Pause. In the pause of the exhale, through your soul essence sphere, greet Earth and ask it to send a stream of energy upward, stopping 19 to 22 inches out in front of you, at nose height. **Inhale.**

Exhale.

Pause. Through your soul essence, greet Sky and ask Sky to drop down a thin strand of energy down to meet a strand of Earth energy.

Regular breath. The two energies will meet and will form the clearing vortex.

If there is anything in the 2nd Vortex that interferes with it being in communication with sensing, release it into the clearing vortex. It is not important that you understand what sensing or being in communication with sensing means. You will learn this by becoming in communication with sensing through your emergence into the body.

Regular breath. Focus each time in the pause of the breath, allowing the clearing vortex to do its work. Attract and draw, from your 2nd Vortex, what is not in alignment with sensing in the 2nd Vortex.

During the clearing, if you feel uncomfortable, adjust your Earth and Sky flow. From the center of your head and your soul essence sphere, ask if you need to increase or decrease the amount of energy to support you in your practice. Remember that you can release feelings or uncomfortable body feelings down your grounding corridor into the flow of mantle.

When complete, the vortex will close and the energy will dissipate.

Clear Grief

Exhale.

Pause. In the pause of the exhale, connect thumb to pinky finger.

Ask from the center of your head for a clearing vortex to form on the outside at your aura.

Inhale.

Exhale.

Pause. In the pause of the exhale, through your soul essence sphere, greet Earth and ask it to send a stream of energy up stopping 19 to 22 inches out in front of you, at nose height.

Inhale

Exhale.

Pause. Through your soul essence, greet Sky and ask Sky to drop a thin strand of energy downward to meet a strand of Earth energy.

Regular breath. The two energies will meet and will form the clearing vortex.

From the center of your head, greet your 2nd Vortex and the clearing vortex. Know that grief on a soul level through coming into the experience into human form is one of the toxins that need to be removed from our 2nd Vortex. Allow this grief to leave into the clearing vortex on the outside edge of your aura.

Regular breath. Take six to seven breaths clearing grief. When complete the vortex will close and the energy will dissipate.

Clear Overwhelm

Exhale.
Pause. In the pause of the exhale, create a clearing vortex on the outside edge of your aura.
Inhale.
Exhale.
Pause. In the pause of the exhale, through your soul essence sphere, greet Earth and ask it to send a stream of energy upward, stopping 19 to 22 inches out in front of you, at nose height.
Inhale.
Exhale.
Pause. Through your soul essence, greet Sky and ask Sky to drop a thin strand of energy downward to meet a strand of Earth energy.
Regular breath. The two energies will meet and will form the clearing vortex.

From the center of your head, greet your 2nd Vortex and the feeling of overwhelm.
Be in your practice, supported by Earth flow, Sky flow, and contained by your Breath of Life. Allow the clearing vortex to begin to draw to overwhelm out of your 2nd Vortex.
Inhale. Adjust your practice if you need to.
Know, as overwhelm releases that you are supported by Earth flow, Sky flow, and the container of your own Breath of Life. Know that overwhelm came from not creating boundaries for fear of rejection. This broke your connection to your sense of soul in body and sense of being.
Regular breath. Do three to six breaths, clearing. When complete, the vortex will close and the energy will dissipate.

Clearing Information that is not in Affinity

Exhale.
Pause. In the pause of the exhale, ask your soul essence sphere for a clearing vortex to form.
Inhale.
Exhale.
Pause. In the pause of the exhale, through your soul essence sphere, greet Earth and ask it to send a stream of energy upward, stopping 19 to 22 inches out in front of you, at nose height.
Inhale.
Exhale.
Pause. Through your soul essence, greet Sky and ask Sky to drop a thin strand of energy downward to meet a strand of Earth energy.
Regular breath. The two energies will meet and will form the clearing vortex.
Allow the clearing vortex to clear information out of your 2nd Vortex that is not in affinity with your soul essence knowing.

Regular breath. Do three to six breaths, clearing. When cleared, the vortex will close and the energy will dissipate.

Be with your soul essence sphere in the center of your head and in communication with your sacred space in the still point in the flow of mantle. Know you are supported by Earth flow, Sky flow, and awakened to the knowledge of the sensing core and the ability of your 2nd Vortex.

Your 2nd Vortex is the center of sensing in the body and therefore the center of relationship. The 2nd Vortex dictates your relationship to incoming energies. It also is key to your soul's ability to self-regulate within the human body since it communicates with the flow of energy as food moves through our small intestine. Therefore, the 2nd Vortex gives us a true sense of self and is the first foundational block of knowledge of being in body (sensing).

Exhale.
Pause. In the pause of the exhale, connect thumb to pinky finger. Be with the information you just read about the 2nd Vortex.
Inhale.
Exhale.
Pause. In the pause, be with the information regarding the 2nd Vortex.
Regular breath, be with the information for three to four breaths. When complete, the clearing vortex will close and the energy will dissipate.

Put in Communication with Soul Essence and Sacred Space

Quartz Crystal Seed

Exhale.
Pause. In the pause of the exhale, ask from your soul essence sphere in the center of your head, for a quartz crystal seed to be created on the outside edge of your aura.
Inhale.
Exhale. Supported in your Embodied Practice, ask from the center of your head and from your soul essence sphere, for the words "body sensing" to appear above the quartz crystal seed.
Inhale.
Exhale. When you are ready, ask from the center of your head for the words "body sensing" to drop into the crystal seed. As they drop into the seed, ask for it to change to the vibration of your soul aspect that your body is ready to work from.
The seed will change to pure energy vibration. You may sense, see, or know that it is there. It will move into your 2nd Vortex when ready.
Regular breath. Take three to six breaths until the vibration of body sensing enters your 2nd Vortex.

Charge Sensing in 2nd Vortex

Exhale.
Pause. In the pause of the exhale, connect thumb to pinky finger. Be with the body sensing in your 2nd Vortex.

Inhale. Charge sensing in your 2nd Vortex.
Hold. In the fullness of breath, be with sensing in your 2nd Vortex.
Exhale. Move with body sensing.
Repeat charging breath two to three times.

2nd Vortex Greets Sacred Space in Flow of Mantle

Exhale.
Pause. In the pause of the exhale, allow your soul essence to greet your 2nd Vortex.
Inhale.
Exhale.
Pause. In the pause of the exhale, allow your still point in the flow of mantle to greet your 2nd Vortex.
The 2nd Vortex is the center of sensing in the body. Be with your 2nd Vortex, in communication with all, held by your still point in the flow of mantle, so that your soul can vibrate in the body. Now, call your soul essence to the 2nd Vortex.

Close your practice by following Closing of Practice and Complete Sections in the Supplemental Chapter.

Color of 2nd Vortex

Understanding our Embodied color association from its wave and frequency standpoint was discussed with the 1st Vortex. The point of origin color for the 2nd Vortex is blue. It has high frequency and short wavelength, equivalent to x-rays. This enables us to sense and have field transfer and experience pictures or flashes that our cell membranes can interpret. Blue is also a cool color. Cooling is the organizing part of creation on Earth. Orange is the popular color association for the 2nd Vortex. When the vibration of orange sets the wavelength and frequency of our 2nd Vortex, our ability to maintain our own embodied fields needed for field transfer is taken. This occurs because the shorter wavelength allows too much energy out via the shorter wavelengths, so the 2nd Vortex's ability to hold its own field integrity falls apart.

When the 2nd Vortex is activated with the point of origin color blue, we begin to experience our super powers as humans living life through sensing, holding our own fields.

Practice Segment 12 - Color Activation of 2nd Vortex

Note: Wait one to two weeks after the 2nd Vortex activation prior to doing the color activation.

Begin by opening Embodied Practice by following the Seated Practice, Soul Essence in the Center of the Head, Grounding, Aural, Four-Part Breath, Earth Flow, and Sky Flow in the Supplemental Chapter.

Exhale.

Pause. In the pause of the exhale, connect thumb to pinky finger. Through your soul essence sphere in the center of your head, create a clearing vortex on the outside edge of your aura.

Inhale.

Exhale.

Pause. In the pause of the exhale, through your soul essence sphere, greet Earth and ask it to send a stream of energy upward, stopping 19 to 22 inches out in front of you, at nose height.

Inhale.

Exhale.

Pause. Through your soul essence, greet Sky and ask Sky to drop a thin strand of energy downward to meet a strand of Earth energy.

Regular breath. The two energies will meet and will form the clearing vortex.

From the center of your head, greet your 2nd Vortex.

Be with attracting what the vortex needs to clear (all vortexes are in relationship).

Through your soul essence, ask the clearing vortex to take out whatever blocks your 2nd Vortex from containing the vibration and frequency of blue.

Inhale.

Exhale.

Pause.

Be with attracting what the 2nd Vortex needs to clear. Through your soul essence sphere, ask the clearing vortex to take out whatever blocks your 2nd Vortex from containing the vibration and frequency of blue.

Inhale.

Exhale

Pause. In the pause of the exhale, continue to allow the clearing vortex to pull energy that is blocking the container of your 2nd Vortex.

Without the container and structure in functional form, the true vibration of the 2nd Vortex will not take root.

When the clearing vortex is ready it will close and the energy will dissipate.

If you feel uncomfortable during this clearing, remember to adjust your Earth and Sky flow so that your body is supported in the practice. If you feel anxious, continue to use the settling breath, connect thumb to pinky finger on the pause of the exhale.

Regular breath, working with the clearing vortex for two to three minutes, until you feel the container of the 2nd Vortex.

We now have created the container to hold the functional aspect, which is vibration and frequency of its point of origin color. It is therefore safe to begin to release the strong feelings from our vortex of what occurred - that this did not happen when you were young, like it was meant to.

Exhale.

Pause. In the pause of the exhale, ask for a clearing vortex to form on the outside edge of your aura.

Give yourself two to three Four-Part Breaths.

Exhale.

Pause. In the pause of the exhale, settle into the above information and let it to wash over you.

Regular breath.

As we develop and begin a tender journey, our DNA, cell membranes, vestibular system, lymphatic system, and all other body systems long to be met. Feelings of warmth, security in safe arms and energetic pulse connection emerge that the developing soul craves. This contact, or being met, creates the container of the 2nd Vortex, which will hold the vibration connection energy with Earth.

Give yourself two to three Four-Part Breaths.

Exhale.

Pause. In the pause of the exhale, through your soul essence sphere, greet Earth and ask it to send a stream of energy upward, stopping 19 to 22 inches out in front of you, at nose height.

Inhale.

Exhale.

Pause. Through your soul essence, greet Sky and ask Sky to drop down a thin strand of energy down to meet a strand of Earth energy.

Regular breath. The two energies will meet and will form the clearing vortex.

Pause. In the pause of the exhale, create a clearing vortex on the outside edge of your aura.

Begin to move out feelings from being in the womb of not being pulsed with from the mother or of having to take form without a proper energetic container. Remember to stay in the center of your head with your soul essence sphere as you allow the clearing vortex to absorb and draw those feelings of not being met.

Regular breath. Take two to three minutes releasing into the clearing vortex until it feels complete for now. The clearing vortex will close and the energy will dissipate.

Exhale.

Pause. In the pause of the exhale, allow a droplet of blue to form on the outside edge of your aura - the size of a drop of water.

Inhale.

Exhale.

Pause. In the pause of the exhale, connect thumb to pinky finger. Be with your soul essence sphere in the center of your head. Be with the drop of blue on the outside of your aura.

Inhale. Connect thumb to ring finger. Know the ability to process on a photon light level. Welcome in the vibration and frequency of blue.

Pause. Hold the fullness of breath. Connect thumb to middle finger. Allow the sensing with blue to be.

Exhale. Be with the frequency of blue.

Regular breath, until you feel that you are ready to continue.

Exhale.

Pause. In the pause of the exhale, connect thumb to pinky finger. Through your soul essence sphere, greet the container in the core of your 2nd Vortex.

Inhale. Pulsate down to meet the core of your 2nd Vortex, connect thumb to ring finger.

Pause. Hold in the fullness of breath. Connect thumb to middle finger. Be with the container in your 2nd Vortex.

Exhale.

Pause. In the pause, connect thumb to pointer finger. Invite blue energy to drop into the exact center where the container formed, to accept the vibration and frequency of blue.
Regular breath for one to two minutes

Exhale.
Pause. In the pause, connect thumb to pinky finger. Through your soul essence sphere, greet the container in the core of your 2nd Vortex.
Inhale. Pulsate down to meet the core of your 2nd Vortex, connect thumb to ring finger.
Hold in the fullness of breath middle finger. Be with the container in your 2nd Vortex.
Exhale. On the exhale, connect thumb to pointer finger. Invite blue energy to the exact center where the container forms to the aspect of the vibration and frequency of blue.

Inhale.
Exhale.
Pause. In the pause of the exhale, connect thumb to pinky finger. Think of one simple aspect of your life where you would like to use your sensing abilities. It could be an aspect of your life, an aspect of past, future, or anything.
Exhale.
Pause. In the pause of the exhale, sense through blue frequency and vibration whatever you would like to sense. Give yourself permission in the center of your head to sense what is.
Regular breath. Be with your sensing in your 2nd Vortex.

Close your practice by following Closing of Practice and Complete Sections in the Supplemental Chapter.

Chapter 13

Embodied Body Relationship
The 3rd Vortex

The 3rd Embodied Vortex is the Body Relationship Vortex; it is the point of origin in the meeting between Earth and Sky. Therefore, it is associated with two elements, air and wood. When air and wood meet in the 3rd Vortex, the energy fuels the vortex and the vortex then energetically feeds our DNA and cell signaling in the body. The 3rd Vortex is the point of origin of complete mechanisms of field transfer in the body. Mechanisms such as gene expression and DNA snips turn on and off energetically, regulated by the 3rd Vortex. Protein synthesis, including protein that unravels from our DNA in the aging process, is facilitated through the 3rd Vortex. In addition to Earth and Sky field transfer, this vortex is the radiating powerhouse of protein synthesis.

While the complete complexities of the following example are far beyond the scoop of this book, let's look, simply, at two people exposed to the same environmental radiation: one gets cancer, the other does not. While radiation affects the genetic snips and how genes express themselves, a functioning 3rd Vortex, will continue to self-regulate the mechanisms that determine DNA and gene expression, allowing the positive genetic snips to be left turned on, preventing one person from getting cancer.

Protein synthesis, including protein that unravels from our DNA in the aging process, is facilitated through the 3rd Vortex. A functioning 3rd Vortex slows the unraveling of the DNA and the impacts of aging on the body. In addition to Earth and Sky field transfer, this vortex is the radiating powerhouse of interrelationship.

The ability of the 3rd Vortex to be in its position between Earth and Sky, allowing air and wood to meet, fueling the functioning of all our vortexes, our DNA and cell signaling, is the point of origin of all health within the body. Simply put, if we do not have our 3rd Vortex functioning, allowing the meeting of air and wood, fueling the vortex and feeding our DNA, in its position between Earth and Sky, we are likely to age more quickly, and experience ill health.

Note: As you read about the 3rd Vortex (as wells as the other vortexes), remember that their successful activation and functioning does not depend on your cognitively understanding all of their energetic or biological mechanisms. We can reap all the benefits of our activated 3rd Vortex, whether or not we understand how it works. Ultimately the 3rd Vortex, as all the others, can only be experienced and understood through our sensing. The Practice Segments awaken us to our ability to sense the energy of the vortexes, their containers, their qualities and their position in our daily functioning.

Aspect

The 3rd Embodied Body Relationship Vortex houses three aspects. First, it houses the pulse of the breath. This is both an inward and outward pulse, facilitating one of our connections to the Principle of 4x4 to Infinity. Second, the 3rd Vortex houses the aspects of Earth, the lungs themselves. Third, the 3rd Vortex houses the aspect of Sky, the air from the atmosphere that processes through the lungs.

Abilities

The meeting of Earth and Sky in every breath creates our energetic sleep-body (a field body that mirrors our physical form) when body breathing changes into deep sleep. Whenever two opposite energies meet, another energy is created. When the energies of Earth and Sky meet in the 3rd Vortex, we can experience sleep on a soul level. When we awake, our sleep body returns to our 3rd Vortex and the 3rd Vortex begins sending information from our dreams to the brain to interpret it and aid us in our lives.

Practice Segment 13 - Activation of Body Relationship - The 3rd Vortex

Open your Embodied Practice by following the Seated Practice, Soul Essence in Center of Head, Grounding, Aural, Four-Part Breath, Earth Flow, and Sky Flow from the Supplemental Chapter.

Clearing of 3rd Vortex

Clear Communication Blocks

Ask through your soul essence sphere in the center of your head and create a clearing vortex on the outside edge of your aura.
Exhale.
Pause. In the pause of the exhale, through your soul essence sphere, greet Earth and ask it to send a stream of energy upward, stopping 19 to 22 inches out in front of you, at nose height.
Inhale.
Exhale.
Pause. Through your soul essence sphere, greet Sky and ask Sky to drop a thin strand of energy downward to meet a strand of Earth energy.
Regular breath. The two energies will meet and will form the clearing vortex.
From the center of your head, greet your 3rd Vortex. Your 3rd Vortex is located in your solar plexus, three fingers above your belly button.
Exhale.
Pause. In the pause of the breath, connect thumb to pinky finger. Be with your 3rd Vortex.
Allow your breath to continue. Inhale when you need to and, in every pause, be with your 3rd Vortex.
Regular breath for one minute.
From the center of your head and with your soul essence sphere, greet the clearing vortex you created on the outside edge of your aura.

Begin to release anything in the 3rd Vortex that blocks it from communication through pulse. It is not important that you understand what pulse or being in communication though pulse means - you will learn that as you emerge into the body.

Exhale.

Pause. In the pause of the breath, focus and allow the clearing vortex to do its work. Attract and draw, from your 3rd Vortex, what is not in alignment with pulse in the 3rd Vortex.

During the clearing, if you feel uncomfortable, adjust your Earth and Sky flow. Remember that you can release feelings or uncomfortable body feelings down your grounding corridor into Earth.

Regular breath, allowing the clearing for one to two minutes.

Clear Grief, Rage, or Anxiety

From the center of your head, greet your 3rd Vortex and the clearing vortex. Know that a deep grief, rage, or anxiety may come up about not being able to develop in communication through pulse. You may also experience deep energetic loss of connection to *what is* as a human and how pulse communication inward allows us to remember this.

Regular breath. Take as much time as you need to clear into the clearing vortex. When complete, the vortex will close and the energy will dissipate.

Clear Confusion

Exhale.

Pause. In the pause of the exhale, create a new clearing vortex on the outside edge of your aura.

Inhale.

Exhale.

Pause. In the pause of the exhale, through your soul essence sphere, greet Earth and ask it to send a stream of energy upward, stopping 19 to 22 inches out in front of you, at nose height.

Inhale.

Exhale.

Pause. Through your soul essence sphere, greet Sky and ask Sky to drop a thin strand of energy downward to meet a strand of Earth energy.

Regular breath. The two energies will meet and will form the clearing vortex.

From the center of your head, greet your 3rd Vortex and the feeling of confusion.

Be in your practice, supported by Earth flow, Sky flow, contained by your Breath of Life, and allow the clearing vortex to pull confusion out of your 3rd Vortex.

Adjust your practice if you need to.

Regular breath. Let the words flow over you as you release confusion.

Know, as confusion releases, that you are supported by Earth flow, Sky flow, and the container of your own Breath of Life. Know that confusion has come from not being taught how to communicate through pulse or through the transfer of frequency via changes in electromagnetic fields. Most of us were rejected, punished, left alone, or diagnosed if we tried to explore the pulse relationship with the electromagnetic field of Earth with our own soul, in connection to our soul essence.

Inhale. Connect thumb to ring finger.

Pause. Hold in the fullness of breath. Connect thumb to middle finger.

Exhale. Connect thumb to pointer finger.

Regular breath.

If you need to balance out on a body level you can stretch up to the ceiling or down to the floor, in whatever way is most comfortable for you. You can do this while running your energy and holding your cobalt blue.

Stay with your soul essence sphere.

Settle back, getting comfortable in the chair. Be with your soul essence sphere in the center of your head, in communication with your sacred space in the flow of mantle in Earth. Be supported by Earth iron flow and Sky flow. Awaken to the knowledge of pulse relationship and the abilities of your 3rd Vortex.

Supported by your practice, remember your third vortex is the center of pulse in the body. The third vortex is critical to your soul being able to regulate information in the body, to communicate for you and to also to move energy through the body.

Exhale.

Pause. In the pause of the exhale, connect thumb to pinky finger. Be with the information you just heard, be with your third vortex.

Quartz Crystal Seed

Exhale.

Pause. In the pause of the exhale, ask your soul essence sphere in the center of your head for a quartz crystal seed to form on the outside edge of your aura.

Regular breath. When you are ready, ask from the center of your head and with your soul essence sphere for the word "pulse" to drop into the crystal seed on the outside edge of your aura. As the word 'pulse' drops into the crystal seed, it will change into the vibration that your 3rd Vortex needs to begin to grow and develop into pulse relationship.

Exhale.

Pause. In the pause of the exhale, connect thumb to pinky finger. Allow vibration pulse energy to come to the direct center of your third vortex.

Inhale. Charge the pulse.

Pause. Hold, in the fullness of breath. Be with pulse in your 3rd Vortex.

Exhale. Move sensing flow into pulse.

Regular breath.

Take a moment to be with your third vortex. Remember to adjust your practice as we charge the 3rd Vortex. If your body feels uncomfortable, adjust your grounding and release.

Close your practice by following Closing of Practice and Complete Sections in the Supplemental Chapter.

Color of 3rd Vortex

The point of origin color of the 3rd Vortex is green, which possesses a medium high frequency and shorter wavelength. This communication facilitates an equal energy transfer;

an equal transfer of oxygen and carbon dioxide. The equal transfer is involved in developing our energetic sleep body.

Yellow is the common association color for the 3rd Vortex. Yet, it keeps us from charging our sleep energy body, thus hampering our ability to truly know where we are when we sleep. The human field has constructed energy fields in which our dreams occur, to fool us, to make us think we have traveled somewhere in our sleep, when we have not. Without our balanced sleep field body, we most likely are experiencing a dream within a dream.

Practice Segment 14 - Color Activation of 3rd Vortex

Note: Wait one to two weeks after the 3rd Vortex activation before doing the color activation.

Open your Embodied Practice by following the Seated Practice, Soul Essence in the Center of the Head, Grounding, Aural, Four-Part Breath, Earth Flow, and Sky Flow in the Supplemental Chapter.

Exhale.
Pause. In the pause of the exhale, connect thumb to pinky finger.
Through your soul essence sphere in the center of your head, create a clearing vortex on the outside edge of your aura.
Exhale.
Pause. In the pause of the exhale, through your soul essence sphere, greet Earth and ask it to send a stream of energy upward, stopping 19 to 22 inches out in front of you, at nose height.
Inhale.
Exhale.
Pause. Through your soul essence sphere, greet Sky and ask Sky to drop a thin strand of energy downward to meet a strand of Earth energy.

Regular breath. The two energies will meet and will form the clearing vortex.
From the center of your head, greet your 3rd Vortex.
Through your soul essence, ask the dandelion to pull whatever is blocking your 3rd Vortex from being the container that it needs to hold the vibration and frequency of green, its point of origin color vibration.
Exhale.
Pause. In the pause of the exhale, continue to allow the clearing vortex to pull energy that blocks the container of your 3rd Vortex.
Reminder, without the container and structure in functional form, the true vibration of the 3rd Vortex will not take root.
Regular breath.
If you feel uncomfortable during this clearing, remember to adjust your Earth and Sky flow so that your body is supported in the practice. If you feel anxious, continue to use your Settling Breath, connecting thumb to pinky on the pause of the exhale.
Regular breath.

We have created the container to hold the functional aspect, which is vibration and frequency. Now it is safe to begin to release the strong feelings that emerged from our 3rd Vortex of what did not occur – that the energetic structure and container of the 3rd Vortex did not form as it was meant to, when you were young.

Exhale.
Pause. Be with your soul essence pulse in the center of your head,
Inhale.
Exhale.
Pause. Connect thumb to pinky.
Inhale. Move thumb to ring finger.
Pause in the fullness of breath, middle finger.
Exhale. Move thumb to index finger.
Repeat four times.
Regular breath.

The opening of the diaphragm is a physical combination of the muscle structure and fascia that gives us strength to walk and stand in position between Earth and Sky. The soul essence comes into communication and moves into the 3rd Vortex, setting the energetic boundary, allowing each of us to stand in our magnificence. This facilitates saying "no" to things that are energetically intrusive. When the child's magnificence and their "no" are respected by the parent(s), the diaphragm develops the ability to relax downward with each breath. This relaxation downward gives use to the balanced energy transfer of oxygen and carbon dioxide, which is the blueprint for other energetic transfers in the body. If this does not occur, the soul essence doesn't feel safe to establish this opening.
Release grief.
When you feel complete the vortex will close. The feelings and the energy will dissipate.

Charging the 3rd Vortex

Exhale.
Pause. In the pause of the exhale, allow a green droplet to form on the outside edge of your aura - the size of a drop of water.
Inhale.
Exhale.
Pause. In the pause of the exhale, connect thumb to pinky. Be with your soul essence in the center of your head. Be with the dot of green on the outside of your aura.
Inhale. Connect thumb to ring finger. Know the properties of being the container in which field transfer occurs, through the vibration and frequency of green.
Pause. In the fullness of breath, connect thumb to middle finger. Allow pulse with green to be.
Exhale. Be in relationship to the frequency of green.
Inhale.
Exhale.
Pause. In the pause of the exhale, connect thumb to pinky. Through your soul essence pulse, greet the container in the core of your 3rd Vortex.

Inhale. From your soul essence sphere, pulsate down to meet the core of your 3rd Vortex.

Pause. Hold in the fullness of breath. Connect thumb to middle finger. Be with the container in your 3rd Vortex.

Exhale. On the exhale, connect thumb to pointer finger. Invite the green energy to the exact center where the container formed, to accept the vibration and frequency of green.

Regular breath. Be with the vibration of green in the 3rd Vortex for two to three minutes.

Exhale.

Pause. In the pause of the exhale, connect thumb to pinky finger. Let yourself sense with your 3rd Vortex using the vibration of green – and sense what part of your body needs communication through field transfer.

Inhale.

Exhale.

Pause. In the pause of the exhale, be in field transfer through green frequency and vibration, and send energy to that part of your body. Give yourself permission in the center of your head and with your soul essence sphere to sense that change has occurred.

Regular breath.

Be with your soul essence pulse in the center of your head and in communication with your sacred space in the center of Earth, supported by Earth flow and Sky flow, awakened to the knowledge of field transfer and the ability of your 3rd Vortex.

Your 3rd Vortex is the center of field transfer in the body and therefore the center of pulse in the body. The 3rd Vortex dictates relationship by organizing the energy in the body, keeping us in a healthy position to be in relationship to our bodies.

Exhale.

Pause. In the pause of the exhale, connect thumb to pinky finger. Be with the information you have just heard about the 3rd Vortex.

Regular breath, be with the information for one to two minutes.

Be In Communication with Soul Essence and Sacred Space

Exhale.

Pause. In the pause of the exhale, ask your soul essence sphere in the center of your head for a quartz crystal to be created on the outside edge of your aura.

When you are ready, from the center of your head and with your soul essence sphere, ask for the words "Pulse Field Transfer" to drop into the quartz crystal. As the words drop into the quartz crystal, ask for them to change to the vibration of the aspect that your body is ready to work from. The quartz crystal will change to pure energy vibration. You may sense, see, or know that it is there. It will move into your 3rd Vortex.

Exhale.

Pause. In the pause of the exhale, connect thumb to pinky finger. Be with the pulse field transfer relationship in your 3rd Vortex.

Inhale. Charge pulse in your 3rd Vortex.

Pause. In the fullness of breath, be with pulse field transfer in your 3ʳᵈ Vortex.
Exhale. Move with pulse.
Regular breath. Be with pulse field transfer in the 3ʳᵈ Vortex for one to two minutes.

Exhale.
Pause. In the pause of the exhale, allow your soul essence to greet your 3ʳᵈ Vortex.
Regular breath.
Proceed at your own pace. Allow your sacred space in the center of Earth to greet your 3ʳᵈ Vortex.

The 3ʳᵈ Vortex is in communication with your soul essence sphere, in communication with your sacred space in the center of Earth and in pulse field transfer relationship with every breath. The 3ʳᵈ Vortex provides the container within the body's form of balanced chi flow within the body and the communication through pulse field transfer, ever supported with each breath. We awaken the 3ʳᵈ Vortex to be in perfect balance between Earth and Sky.

Close your practice by following Closing of Practice and Complete Sections in the Supplemental Chapter.

Chapter 14

Embodied Field Sphere
The 4th Vortex

Our 4th Embodied Vortex Field Sphere is our most complicated and it takes the longest to develop fully. For the 4th to fully form, we must gather photon light footprints of each past life incarnation. The soul essence past life soul footprints builds the structures of the 4th Vortex.

The 4th Vortex element is photon light. This Vortex gives us the ability to collect and then understand information, which comes in photon light form. Upon death, all the bio-photon light gets released. The biophoton light contains all of the information from the soul which life created in communication with the soul essence. As the biophoton light is released, it organizes into the structure of that soul's life. At this point, the biophoton light is organized in the human field to wait for the soul essence to create another body. In each life, if we learn to gather the biophoton light we left for ourselves in our last life (our past life footprint) to our vortexes in our current life, we create the energetic structures in our 4th Vortex. These are the keys to open the door and connect us across time and space on a soul essence level.

Aspect

The 4th Vortex aspect is a field generator. Our biological heart and vascular system create an aural container in which Embodied Vortexes develop. The field of the heart is formed by the iron in our blood circulating through our closed vascular system. Let's quickly go back to the development of the heart as talked about in Chapter 5. The electromagnetic field of the heart begins at five weeks of gestation, when the two chambers of the heart begin to contain, and blood flow begins in the developing baby. This field begins the blocking from communication with soul essence, as the soul body forms through the ability. The soul essence waits for the soul to develop in body to reestablish its energetic connections.

Abilities

There are two core abilities of the 4th Field Sphere Vortex. The first core ability is the capacity to be in affinity with self and with others. The correct position, structure, and container in the 4th Vortex facilitate this ability. When the 4th Vortex is completely developed, the second core ability is our connection to the fibrous strands of space, which house our soul essence line or our connection to our soul pool's position on Earth.

Practice Segment 15 - Activation of Field Sphere - The 4th Vortex

Open your Embodied Practice by following the Seated Practice, Soul Essence in Center of Head, Grounding, Aural, Four-Part Breath, Earth Flow, and Sky Flow from the Supplemental Chapter.

Clearing of Container of 4th Vortex

Exhale.

Pause. In the pause, connect thumb to pinky finger. Through your soul essence sphere in the center of your head, create a clearing vortex on the outside edge of your aura.

Inhale.

Exhale.

Pause. In the pause of the exhale, through your soul essence sphere, greet Earth and ask it to send a stream of energy upward, stopping 19 to 22 inches out in front of you, at nose height.

Inhale.

Exhale.

Pause. Through your soul essence sphere, greet Sky and ask Sky to drop a thin strand of energy downward to meet a strand of Earth energy.

Regular breath. The two energies will meet and will form the clearing vortex.

From the center of your head, greet your 4th Vortex. Your 4th Vortex is slightly to the left (by one to two fingers) of your sternum.

Inhale.

Exhale.

Pause. In the pause of the breath, connect thumb to pinky finger. Be with your 4th Vortex.

Allow your breath to continue. Inhale when you need to and, in every pause, be with your 4th Vortex.

Inhale.

Pause. In the pause of the inhale, connect thumb to pinky finger. Support being with your 4th Vortex.

Be with regular breath, settling in the pause of the exhale each time for one to two minutes.

Clear Communication Blockages

Exhale.

Pause. From the center of your head and with your soul essence sphere, greet the clearing vortex you created on the outside edge of your aura.

Regular breath.

Begin to release anything in the 4th Vortex that blocks it from communication with the container of affinity. It is not important that you understand what the container of affinity is in order to be with it.

Focus. In the pause of the breath, allow the clearing vortex to do its work. Attract and draw, from your 4th Vortex, what is not in alignment with the container in the 4th Vortex.

During the clearing, if you feel uncomfortable, adjust your Earth and Sky flow. Remember that you can release feelings or uncomfortable body feelings down your grounding corridor into Earth.

Allow the clearing vortex to do its work and continue to clear a space for the container of affinity to emerge.

Exhale.

Pause. In the pause of the exhale, connect thumb to pinky finger.

From the center of your head and with your soul essence sphere, greet your 4th Vortex and the clearing vortex. Know and sense (beyond words) that what is leaving is confusion and loss for the true nature of your soul essence. Sense the connected fibers that first awakened us and then the force that kicked us out of our container of affinity across time and space. Allow whatever comes up to be pulled into the clearing vortex on the outside edge of your aura.

Continue to work with regular breath.

Exhale.

Pause. In the pause of the exhale, create a clearing vortex on the outside edge of your aura.

From the center of your head and with your soul essence sphere, greet your 4th Vortex and the feeling of emptiness.

Regular breath.

Be in your practice, supported by Earth and Sky flow, contained by your Breath of Life. Allow the clearing vortex to begin to pull out your 4th Vortex emptiness.

Adjust your practice if you need to.

Know, as it releases, you are supported by Earth flow, Sky flow, and the container of your own Breath of Life. The sense of loss beyond words began when the most connected container of who we are on a soul-body level was labeled and treated as a pump, not a container for sensing and creation. This knowledge and treatment of our 4th Vortex as a pump has broken our connections to our soul DNA. Be in your practice, supported by Earth and Sky flow. Be with this information, that we must hear and clear the information that labeled our 4th Vortex as a pump, allowing us to reclaim our container of affinity.

Clear Grief, Anxiety, and/or Rage

Allow it to begin to clear grief and rage out of your 4th Vortex, which has come from being treated a pump.

Be with your soul essence sphere in the center of your head and in communication with your sacred space in the center of Earth, supported by Earth and Sky flow, and awakened to the container of being.

Take a moment to be with the information that your 4th Vortex and your physical heart are containers. The physical heart is the structure that monitors balanced (blood pressure) flow and senses what is in the blood.

Exhale.

Pause. In the pause of the exhale, connect thumb to pinky finger. Be with the information you have just heard about the 4th Vortex.

Inhale.

Exhale.

Pause. In the pause, be with the information regarding the 4th Vortex.

Regular breath.

Continue to be with the information for two to three minutes. The clearing vortex will close and the energy will dissipate, when it is ready.

Quartz Crystal Seed

Exhale.
Pause. In the pause of the exhale, ask from your soul essence sphere in the center of your head for a quartz crystal seed to be created on the outside edge of your aura.
Supported in your Embodied Practice, from the center of your head and with your soul essence sphere, ask for the words "field generator" to appear above the quartz crystal in word form.
When you are ready, from the center of your head, ask for the words "field generator" to drop into the quartz crystal seed. As it drops into the quartz crystal seed, ask for it to change to the vibration of your soul essence aspect that your body is ready to work from.
The quartz crystal will change to pure energy vibration. You may sense, see, or know that it is there. It will move into your 4th Vortex.

Put in Communication with Soul Essence and Sacred Space

Exhale.
Pause. In the pause of the exhale, connect thumb to pinky finger. Be with the container in your 4th Vortex.
Inhale. Charge the container in your 4th Vortex.
Pause. In the fullness of breath, be with the container in your 4th Vortex.
Exhale. Move out from the container of the soul.
Repeat three to four times.

Exhale.
Pause. In the pause of the exhale, allow your soul essence to greet your 4th Vortex.
Inhale.
Exhale.
Pause. In the pause of the exhale, allow your sacred space in the center of Earth to greet your 4th Vortex.
The 4th Vortex is the container of soul relationship across time and space and is in communication with the spaces where the pulse fields move back and forth, creating life.

Close your practice by following Closing of Practice and Complete Sections in the Supplemental Chapter.

Color of 4th Vortex

The Field Sphere Vortex point of origin color is red. Red has a low frequency and longer wavelength. Red is associated with the infrared light. In this range of light, information can flow in, yet block out or reflect certain frequencies. The properties of red support the container of the heart and protection for the soul's photon light. Without this protection, the soul essence will not gather its past life footprints. We see this when the 4th Vortex is activated to the commonly associated color green. The wavelength and frequency properties of the color green transfer energy. But the soul essence wants domain over its own light; it doesn't want to share or transfer its energy. So, when the 4th Vortex is pulsing with green, it doesn't gather past life footprints.

Practice Segment 16 - Color Activation of the 4th Vortex

Note: Wait one to two weeks after 4th Vortex activation before doing color activation.

Open your Embodied Practice by following the Seated Practice, Soul Essence in the Center of the Head, Grounding, Aural, Four-Part Breath, Earth Flow, and Sky Flow in the Supplemental Chapter.

Exhale.
Pause. In the pause of the exhale, connect thumb to pinky.
Through your soul essence sphere in the center of your head, create a clearing vortex on the outside edge of your aura.
Inhale.
Exhale.
Pause. In the pause of the exhale, through your soul essence sphere, greet Earth and ask it to send a stream of energy upward, stopping 19 to 22 inches out in front of you, at nose height.
Inhale.
Exhale.
Pause. Through your soul essence sphere, greet Sky and ask Sky to drop a thin strand of energy downward to meet a strand of Earth energy.
Regular breath. The two energies will meet and will form the clearing vortex.

Inhale.
From the center of your head, greet your 4th Vortex.
Through your soul essence, ask the clearing vortex to pull whatever blocks your 4th Vortex from being the container to hold the vibration and frequency of red, its point of origin color vibration.
Regular breath.
Exhale. In the pause of the exhale, continue to allow the clearing vortex to pull energy that is blocking the container of your 4th Vortex.
Without the field sphere in functional form, the true vibration of the 4th Vortex will not take root.
Regular breath.
If you feel uncomfortable during this clearing, remember to adjust your Earth and Sky flow so that your body is supported in the practice. If you feel anxious, continue to use the Settling Breath, connecting thumb to pinky finger in the pause of the exhale.
Regular breath, clearing one to two minutes.

We have created the container of the 4th Vortex to hold the functional aspect, which is vibration and frequency. Now it is safe to release the strong feelings that emerged from our 4th Vortex of what did not occur – that this did not happen when you were young, like it was meant to.

Exhale.
Pause. Be with your soul essence sphere in the center of your head,

Inhale.

Exhale.

Pause. Connect thumb to pinky finger.

Inhale. Connect thumb to ring finger.

Pause. In the fullness of breath, connect thumb to middle finger.

Exhale. Connect thumb to index finger.

Repeat two to three times.

Affinity with self cannot be attained by changing our cognitive thoughts through thought monitoring. Affinity comes over time as we develop and gather our photon light energy to our 4th Vortex, thus giving our human experience connection across time and space. This connection also brings us into affinity with others.

Exhale.

Pause. Settle into the pause, continue clearing.

Permission to know what information or occurrences blocked you from developing and connecting to affinity with self.

Regular breath. Allow clearing for two to three minutes into the clearing vortex. When complete for the time being, it will close and the energy will dissipate.

Exhale.

Pause. In the pause of the exhale, allow a red droplet to form on the outside edge of your aura - the size of a drop of water.

Exhale

Pause. In the pause of the exhale, connect thumb to pinky. Be with your soul essence in the center of your head with your soul essence sphere. Be with the dot of red on the outside of your aura.

Inhale. Connect thumb to ring finger.

Pause. In the fullness of breath, connect thumb to middle finger. Allow the sensing container to prepare for the frequency of red.

Exhale. Contain the frequency of red.

Inhale.

Exhale.

Pause. In the pause of the exhale, be with your 4th Vortex and the droplet of red.

Inhale.

Exhale.

Pause. In the pause of the exhale, connect thumb to pinky finger. Through your soul essence sphere, greet the container in the core of your 4th Vortex.

Inhale. Pulsate down to meet the core of your 4th Vortex.

Pause. In the fullness of breath, connect thumb to middle finger. Be with the container in your 4th Vortex.

Exhale. On the exhale, connect thumb to pointer finger. Invite the red energy to the exact center where the container formed, to accept the vibration and frequency of red.

Regular breath. If you feel that you need to, adjust your flow of energy while keeping your sacrum charged with Breath of Life.

Exhale.

Pause. In the pause of the exhale, connect thumb to pinky finger. Let your heart sense what is. Take five to ten pauses to sense.

Exhale.

Take two to three minutes to now just be in your practice with 4th Vortex vibration and frequency utilized now.

Close your practice by following Closing of Practice and Complete Sections in the Supplemental Chapter.

Chapter 15

Embodied Unseen
The 5th Vortex

The point of origin in physical form of the 5th Unseen Vortex originates between the cervical and the 1st thoracic vertebrae. The element of the 5th Vortex is fire, the space between the point of origin of creation. The sun's mass creates gravity, which interfaces with the mass of the planets, and determines the spaces in between which allows the solar system to be.

Aspect

The 5th Unseen Vortex, in the early years of my awakening to Embodiment was my favorite vortex. For me, it was the easiest to use. Some of you will find it the hardest to use and others will be somewhere in between. It was my favorite because it had many different aspects and it was effective in working with other people. Simply using the voice connected to the heart, the 5th Vortex can completely change something. Even though we may not know at the time what the mechanisms are that we are working with, it is the space in between our tones, not the tone. This space between our tones can only form when the 4th Vortex is connected to the 5th Vortex.

The aspect of the 5th Vortex is the space in between which has been talked about in many ways and is understood in just as many ways. There are limitless, probably infinite levels of function within the space in between, in space and here on Earth.

For example, the atom, the building block of all matter (and thus life) is on Earth so we can experience it. It is a very simple structure that contains a nucleus, charged protons, and neutrons (which do not hold a charge). Around the nucleus are electrons that also hold a charge. The holding of positive charges, negative charges, and the mass relationships create the space, which makes the structure of the atoms. Without the ability of the negative and positive charges to hold the space there would be no atoms.

It is the space that allows the structure to be and the amount of space that contributes to the shape of structure. On the larger end of examples, we have our solar system or the Universe. Each galaxy and each solar system is very much dedicated in the space it occupies. It is not just six, nine, or twelve planets, it is the amount of space and distances between each planet (and all the other bodies) and the orbit of each planet around the star and the sun or suns of each solar system that dictates how that solar system will present itself and function.

Abilities

There are four general abilities in the 5th Unseen Vortex. The ability of clairaudience is the ability to translate the wave and frequency patterns (the spaces in between the waves) into human words or understanding. Most other species exclusively communicate through a singular ability. Second, our inner voice is extremely advanced because it is literally the ability to know what the spaces in the body mean or if the spaces of the structures in body are correct. The third is the whisper of the soul essence. Our past life footprint will whisper to us through our 5th Vortex to awaken us and help us to find our soul's photon light footprints so we can gather and be complete in each incarnation. The fourth ability of the 5th Vortex is to set a vibration or frequency within the body and aid in pulsing with whatever electromagnetic fields the body finds itself in.

Practice Segment 17 - Activation of Unseen - The 5th Vortex

Open your Embodied Practice by following the Seated Practice, Soul Essence in Center of Head, Grounding, Aural, Four-Part Breath, Earth Flow, and Sky Flow from the Supplemental Chapter.

Clearing of Unseen

Exhale.
Pause. In the pause of the exhale, through your soul essence sphere in the center of your head, ask to create a clearing vortex on the outside edge of your aura.
Inhale.
Exhale.
Pause. In the pause of the exhale, through your soul essence sphere, greet Earth and ask it to send a stream of energy upward, stopping 19 to 22 inches out in front of you, at nose height.
Inhale.
Exhale.
Pause. Through your soul essence sphere, greet Sky and ask Sky to drop a thin strand of energy downward to meet a strand of Earth energy.
Regular breath. The two energies will meet and will form the clearing vortex.

From the center of your head and with your soul essence sphere, greet your 5th Vortex. Your 5th Vortex is located at the base of your throat.
Regular breath.
Exhale.
Pause. In the pause of the breath, connect thumb to pinky finger. Be with your 5th Vortex.
Allow your breath to continue. Inhale when you need to and, in every pause, be with your 5th Vortex.
Continue this for one to two minutes.

Exhale.
Pause. Begin to release anything in the 5th Vortex that interferes with it being in communication with vibration. It is not important that you understand what vibration or being in communication with the vibration means - you will learn that through being in communication with vibration through emergence into the body.
Inhale.

Pause. Focus, in the pause of the breath, allowing the clearing vortex to do its work. Attract and draw from your 5th Vortex what is not in alignment with vibration in the 5th Vortex. During the clearing, if you feel uncomfortable, adjust your Earth and sky flow. Remember that you can release emotions or uncomfortable body feelings down your grounding corridor into Earth.

Exhale.

Pause. In the pause of the exhale, connect thumb to pinky finger.

From the center of your head, create a clearing vortex on the outside edge of your aura.

Inhale. Allow the clearing vortex to once again do its work and continue to clear lack of communication with vibration.

Clear Grief or Rage

Exhale.

Pause. In the pause of the exhale, connect thumb to pinky. From the center of your head and with your soul essence sphere, greet your 5th Vortex and begin releasing any deep rage or grief about things being jammed into your 5th Vortex. Think of a violin or guitar jammed with cotton. When the strings are plucked by the soul body, they cannot sound. Allow whatever comes up to move into the clearing vortex.

Regular breath, take one to two minutes clearing.

Clear Emptiness

From the center of your head, greet your 5th Vortex and the feeling of emptiness.

Be in your practice, supported by Earth flow, Sky flow, contained by your Breath of Life, and allow the clearing vortex to begin to pull out of your 5th Vortex emptiness.

Adjust your practice if you need to.

Know, as it is releasing and as you are supported by Earth flow, Sky flow, and the container of your own Breath of Life that the emptiness has come from the loss of our own tone, like our own song. No one else's song could or would ever fill the emptiness.

Clearing, take one to two minutes.

Clear What's not in Affinity

Exhale.

Pause. In the pause of the exhale, allow the clearing vortex to begin to clear information out of your 5th Vortex that is not in affinity with your soul essence knowing.

Be with these words as you continue to allow the clearing vortex to clear what is not with soul knowing.

Be with your soul essence sphere in the center of your head and in communication with your sacred space in the center of Earth, supported by Earth flow, Sky flow, and awakened to the knowledge of vibration relationship and the ability of your 5th Vortex.

Your 5th Vortex is the space in between, the space of vibratory relationship and knowledge, the space that allows us to connect to certain fields - to hear and speak our soul whisper.

131

Inhale.
Exhale.
Pause. In the pause of the exhale, connect thumb to pinky finger. Be with the information you have just heard about the 5th Vortex.
Inhale.
Exhale.
Pause. In the pause of the exhale, be with the information regarding the 5th Vortex. Be with this for one to two minutes.

Activating the Aspect of the 5th Vortex

Quartz Crystal Seed

Exhale.
Pause. In the pause of the exhale, from your soul essence sphere in the center of your head, ask for a quartz crystal to be created on the outside edge of your aura.
Regular breath.
Supported in your Embodied Practice, from the center of your head and with your soul essence sphere, ask for the words "space between vibration", to appear above the quartz seed.
When you are ready, from the center of your head and with your soul essence sphere, ask for the words "space between vibration", to drop into the quartz seed. As the words drop into the quartz seed, ask for the words to change to the vibration of your soul aspect that your body is ready to work from.
The crystal seed will change to pure energy vibration. You may sense, see, or know that it is there. It will move into your 5th Vortex in a moment or two.

Charge Vibration in the 5th Vortex

Exhale.
Pause. In the pause of the exhale, connect thumb to pinky finger. Be with the vibratory relationship in your 5th Vortex.
Inhale. Charge vibration in your 5th Vortex.
Hold. In the fullness of breath, be with vibration in your 5th Vortex.
Exhale. Move and sense with vibration.
Repeat this Four-Part Breath two to five times.

Put into Communication with Soul Essence and Still Point

Exhale. In the pause of the exhale, allow your soul essence to greet your 5th Vortex.
On the next pause of the exhale, you can go at your own pace, allow your still point in flow of mantle in the center of Earth to greet your 5th Vortex.
Regular breath.
The 5th Vortex, the center of vibration in the body, in communication with all, held by your sacred space in the center of Earth and the center of your head - so that your soul can vibrate through physical form.

Close your practice by following Closing of Practice and Complete Sections in the Supplemental Chapter.

Color of 5th Vortex

The point of origin color in the 5th Vortex is orange. The color of orange has a lower frequency and longer wavelengths. There is more space between the waves, so the 5th can block vibrations if needed. This is the frequency of broadcast waves; they travel a long way but can be blocked easily. This is a great benefit to the soul for self-protection so one is not seduced by other people's words. I see this over and over again when someone's 5th is set on the frequency and wavelength of the common color associated with blue in the 5th. A teacher or guru can then teach them in ways to move them from communication with their soul essence. Because the soul cannot block the words in the 5th Vortex, the person is overtaken.

Practice Segment 18 - Color Activation of the 5th Vortex

Note: Wait one to two weeks after vortex activation before doing color activation.

Begin by opening Embodied Practice by following the Seated Practice, Soul Essence in the Center of the Head, Grounding, Aural, Four-Part Breath, Earth Flow, and Sky Flow in the Supplemental Chapter.

Exhale.
Pause. In the pause of the exhale, connect thumb to pinky finger.
Through your soul essence pulse in the center of your head, create a clearing vortex on the outside edge of your aura.
Regular breath.
Inhale.
Exhale.
Pause. In the pause of the exhale, through your soul essence sphere, greet Earth and ask it to send a stream of energy upward, stopping 19 to 22 inches out in front of you, at nose height.
Inhale.
Exhale.
Pause. Through your soul essence sphere, greet Sky and ask Sky to drop a thin strand of energy downward to meet a strand of Earth energy.
Regular breath. The two energies will meet and will form the clearing vortex.

Inhale.
From the center of your head, greet your 5th Vortex.
Through your soul essence, ask the clearing vortex to whatever blocks your 5th Vortex from being the container it needs to hold the vibration and frequency of the point of origin color vibration, orange.
Exhale.
Pause. In the pause of the exhale, continue to allow the clearing vortex to pull energy that blocks the container of your 5th Vortex.

Note: Without the container and structure in functional form, the true vibration of the 5th Vortex will not take root.

Regular breath.

If you feel uncomfortable during this clearing, remember to adjust your Earth and Sky flow so that your body is supported in the practice. If you feel anxious, continue to use the Settling Breath on the pause of the exhale, and connect thumb to pinky.

Continue to clear for one to two minutes.

Now that you have created the space in between to hold the functional aspect, which is vibration and frequency, it is safe to begin to release the strong feelings from your vortex of what occurred - that this did not happen when you were young, like it was meant to.

Exhale.

Pause. Be with your soul essence sphere in the center of your head,

Inhale.

Exhale.

Pause. Connect thumb to pinky finger.

Inhale. Connect thumb to ring finger.

Pause. In the fullness of breath, connect thumb to middle finger.

Repeat two to three times.

Regular breath, and let the words wash over you.

Stay with whatever emerged for you during this clearing. Maybe, you sensed that other vortex supports were not given or had not occurred, or your attempt to put out or create something in your life never occurred. Experience the mind-body split, any feelings that emerge, or anything else that comes up. Remember to stay in the center of your head with your soul essence sphere, as you allow the clearing vortex to absorb and draw those feelings of not being able to emerge.

When complete the clearing vortex will close and the energy will dissipate.

Exhale.

Pause. In the pause of the exhale, allow an orange droplet to form on the outside edge of your aura - the size of a drop of water.

Inhale.

Exhale.

Pause. In the pause of the exhale, connect thumb to pinky. Be with your soul essence sphere in the center of your head. Be with the dot of orange on the outside of your aura.

Inhale. Connect thumb to ring finger. Know the mechanism of integration, through the vibration and frequency of orange.

Pause. In the fullness of breath, connect thumb to middle finger. Allow the oneness of mind and body through the frequency of orange.

Exhale.

Repeat above breath two to five times.

Exhale.

Pause. In the pause of the exhale, connect thumb to pinky. Through your soul essence sphere, greet the container in the core of your 5th Vortex.

Inhale. Pulsate down to meet the core of your 5th Vortex.

Pause. In the fullness of breath, connect thumb to middle finger. Be with the container in your 5th Vortex.

Exhale. On the exhale, connect thumb to pointer finger. Invite the orange energy to the exact center where the container formed, to accept the vibration and frequency of orange.

Inhale.

Exhale.

Pause. In the pause of the exhale, connect thumb to pinky finger. Your mind and body are one; made one by the 5th Vortex, speaking through the vibration of your soul.

Inhale.

Exhale.

Pause. In the pause of the exhale, be in communication through orange frequency and vibration with whatever you would like to communicate with Earth. Give yourself permission in the center of your head with your soul essence sphere to sense that the communication is occurring.

Be with this in practice for two to five minutes.

Close your practice by following Closing of Practice and Complete Sections in the Supplemental Chapter.

Chapter 16

Embodied Soul Essence Access
The 6th Vortex

The 6th Embodied Vortex, the Soul Access Vortex, resides in the physical center of our brains, occupying the space above the third ventricle, and at times, occupying the third ventricle itself.

To locate it in the center of our head, we put one finger on the bridge of our nose in between the eyebrows, draw a line straight back, put a finger above each ear, and draw a line between our two ears where the two lines meet. This is the center of our head! This space is where our soul essence sphere gathers and is the communication center during Embodied Practice. In the 6th Vortex we find ourselves sitting right above the amygdala and right below the thalamus, in one of the waterbeds of the brain known as the third ventricle. Cerebral spinal fluid is made in the waterbeds.

The location of the 6th Vortex is quite significant as we begin to understand what we want, how we want to have the fusion, or begin to understand that there is no body and soul dichotomy (split). In everyone there is a soul essence sphere or communication access point in this position over the amygdala. All of the information that comes in through all our senses goes to the corpus striatum, which then triages the information to other parts of the brain. The information is housed, contained, and supported by the soul essence sphere. This very much changes how all the information coming in is to be sorted in the brain. Because the information is moved through the soul essence sphere, we have a powerful mechanism to increase our ability to interpret all 5,000 signals coming at us during each moment of our lives.

Let's use an example to show how the soul essence contains sensing information. In this example, there is a central location through which all information in a large manufacturing plant is processed. It is the job of the central person to make decisions as to the details of each manufacturing item (price and information) and where in the plant the item is needed or handled. Who would we want in charge of that central location; someone who is familiar with all plant operations or someone they just hired off the street?

Now, let's go back to the soul essence sphere! What abilities or connections do we want to have in the center of our head? Do we want a person who limits themselves to hand-picked information from select others, or a selfish person who is only capable of viewing "what is" only through what affects them alone? What is in control of the control center, the corpus striatum, decides how and where to send the information in the body and what will be produced or created in this life.

As the soul essence is activated, it takes its place as the energy in charge of the control center of your whole being. As one follows the Embodied Practice, our soul essence sphere gathers in the center of our head and becomes a self sustaining photon light sphere that connects us to who we are (our position in communication in time and space). This takes years or even lifetimes, but so worth the discipline to gather back your essence and be in communication. While gathering our soul essence into our soul essence sphere, we are vulnerable to other schools of knowledge - gurus or energies out of body that do not want our essence to take its position at the control center. These other entities want their own sensing information or energy in the center of your head, which then controls what your soul beds bring into form, and ultimately what gets sent where and how things are handled.

In other words, when we lack the soul essence sphere, a kind of a void and limited interpretation exists as the corpus striatum makes decisions about where to sort and send the information. Our behavior, the outcomes of our behavior, and how we perceive the world, all change when we only take in sensing information through another's information or essence.

That is pretty complex. Just let us sense it. It is critical to remember the importance of the 6th Vortex, the position of the center of the head, functioning as our control center (or soul essence sphere) to sense information. When we continuously work with our soul essence sphere, we experience how our brain communicates through bio-photons, unlocking our glia cells activities to further support us in gaining our ability to interpret our 5,000 signals as they come to us.

Aspect

From the developmental aspect, we are born with the 6th Vortex functioning. What does that mean? We see energy and when we are born we possess this ability. This is where humans have developed the understanding that the 6th Vortex is associated with sight. It is not the sight that comes from the optic nerve, it is the sight that comes from the sensing - the body's and the brain's ability to make pictures from the sensing system and the lower parts of the brain.

When we are born this is 100% functional. The baby is seeing with their 6th Vortex. They are seeing the energy of the hospital, the energy of the mother, the energy of the father, the doctor and the nurses, etc. At birth, before their 6th Vortex closes, they can also see the condition of the human field - not so much the condition "of the human race" but the human field, which is the energetic container that all humans are in. They are able to see all of this and are taking it in through the 6th Vortex.

Some of you probably feel, or at least have some sense, that this can be quite an overwhelming moment. It is. The infant's experience of overwhelm depends on what energetic information is available to the infant as they take in their energetic surroundings. We will do a healing on this, because one of the core wounds that happen to most of us is that this first seeing experience with our 6th Vortex is not very nurturing or positive.

Certainly, people are not a hundred percent aware of this. Yet, over the last 30 years we are all reawakening and continue to develop more awareness that the atmosphere or the energy of the space surrounding the birth is very critical. A lot of parents have done much to provide their babies with a very different birth experience than they had themselves.

Do not go into mother-guilt, if you did not provide this for your children; it can be healed through the soul essence sphere.

Abilities

The next thing I want to talk about is the use of this information that we are able to receive with the 6th Vortex. When all our sensing is moving into the space in between the thalamus and the amygdala, we are able to make pictures. This gives us the skill and ability, which historically has been referred to as clairvoyance; we are able to see pictures. When we are able to see pictures from that space in between the thalamus and the amygdala, we are in communication with the 2nd, 3rd, 4th, and 5th Vortexes. We have a connection here where we are receiving this information and seeing pictures in a much fuller way than we would if someone was just showing us a snapshot.

Historically, clairvoyants or people who call themselves that, go by the term "psychic". They use their optic nerve to see photon light pictures. That is a skill and ability of the optic nerve. In awakening to Embodied Practice, we can receive and see the information while in communication with that space in between with the 6th Vortex and the other Vortexes. If we wanted to use our optic nerve to read photon light information, the 6th Vortex would pulse up and out and encompass the optic nerve. The crest of the optic nerve is right above the center of the head. This is where information from both optic nerves meets, crosses, and goes to the opposite sides of the brain. It is that meeting point that is very important in reading the photon light signals. At this point, the 6th Vortex references the information. Without a soul essence sphere, one sees the images using only their optic nerve and there is no cross-referencing of the pictures seen through the rest of the vortexes in communication with the space-time vortex.

I know that this is complicated information. As you awaken to new information about yourself as an energetic being, it is important to have a little understanding about the function and structure of the 6th Vortex. Remember, it is not important that you have complete cognitive understanding of this now. That only emerges over time as we experience and integrate the Embodied healings through our soul essence.

Soul Essence and Stress

The position of the 6th Vortex in the brain and its connection to the soul essence sphere is very critical in sleep.

When we are out of communication with our soul essence pulse, the brain will often interpret things that are happening with a much higher degree of stress and anxiety. Even if we do not feel these feelings (maybe we do not show them on the outside or do not know what stress feels like), it does not mean that they are not happening energetically.

A lot of men and women admit they think they are never stressed or do not have any anxieties or worries even in their workday or community involvement. They are often times the same people that report that they are not sleeping. If we are not sleeping, our stress response is part of the problem. The stress response is extremely complicated. Let us focus on a simple part of it, a neural hormone called melatonin and the neural transmitter, acetylcholine. Melatonin and acetylcholine sit opposite each other in the brain. In other words, they are on either side of a little balance scale.

For this example, acetylcholine is excitatory and melatonin is the sleep-inducing signal. Our bodies can produce a lot of acetylcholine because of how we interpret incoming signals. The information enters the brain, gets sorted in the corpus striatum, and fires off a fight or flight response. This sensing information coming through that part of the brain sorts the information and dictates a response.

If something has happened and is interpreted through soul essence, we are much less likely to fire off a fight or flight response. We do not end up in this arena where we ultimately produce too much acetylcholine, which is very agitating. Some acetylcholine is needed to stay alert, have a good functioning memory, and to be present or social. But, when there is too much acetylcholine present, the melatonin cannot increase enough to meet the level of the acetylcholine. As a result, the brain does not balance, stays too agitated, and the body cannot sleep.

In terms of our topic, lack of sleep inhibits the growth of the 6th Vortex. Now, let's see how this is interrelated. We need to have our soul essence sphere in the center of our head so the 6th Vortex can function. If we do not have it there, it cannot modulate and help us triage the information in a different way to avoid too high of a stress response. Then we cannot get good sleep at night. If we do have our soul essence sphere in the center of our head, the 6th Vortex can function. We can reach a state of good sleep, which can help us connect to the levels of the atmosphere that we connect to through our halo Vortex and the brain can heal. Then we can spend time in a patterned sleep state and our 6th Vortex develops through those connections, swimming in the rhythms of the night.

Practice Segment 19 - Activation of Soul Access - The 6th Vortex

Open your Embodied Practice by following the Seated Practice, Soul Essence in Center of Head, Grounding, Aural, Four-Part Breath, Earth Flow, and Sky Flow from the Supplemental Chapter.

Clearing of 6th Vortex

Exhale.
Pause. In the pause of the exhale, through your soul essence sphere in the center of your head, create a clearing vortex on the outside edge of your aura.
Inhale.
Exhale.
Pause. In the pause of the exhale, through your soul essence sphere, greet Earth and ask it to send a stream of energy upward, stopping 19 to 22 inches out in front of you, at nose height.
Inhale.
Exhale.

Pause. Through your soul essence sphere, greet Sky and ask Sky to drop a thin strand of energy downward, to meet a strand of Earth energy.

Regular breath. The two energies will meet and will form the clearing vortex.

Inhale. Soul essence sphere pulses out to meet your 6th Soul Access Vortex. Your 6th Vortex is located in the third ventricle, physical center of the head.

Exhale. Soul essence sphere pulses in like a heartbeat.

Pause. Greet your 6th Vortex, one of the containers of your soul essence pulse sphere.

Inhale.

Exhale.

Pause. In the pause of the breath, connect thumb to pinky finger. Be with your 6th Vortex.

Allow your breath to continue.

Inhale when you need to and, in every pause, be with your 6th soul access Vortex.

Regular breath.

From the center of your head, greet the clearing vortex you created on the outside edge of your aura.

The clearing vortex will begin to clear confusion about what was seen at birth, grief if anything is seen, and/or grief at the change in the human field. Allow the clearing, so that the 6th Vortex can form.

Focus, in the pause of the breath and allow the clearing vortex to do its work. Attract and draw, from your 6th Vortex what is not in alignment with seeing in the 6th Vortex.

During the clearing, if you feel uncomfortable, adjust your Earth and Sky flow. Remember that you can release feelings or uncomfortable body feelings down your grounding corridor into Earth.

Exhale.

Pause. In the pause of the exhale, connect thumb to pinky finger.

Regular breath. Continue to clear for one to two minutes.

Exhale.

Pause. In the pause of the exhale, connect thumb to pinky finger.

From the center of your head, greet your 6th Vortex and the clearing vortex. Begin to clear if you have any deep rage or grief about things seen with the 6th Vortex that cause it to close or to not function correctly. Allow whatever comes up to be pulled into the clearing vortex on the outside edge of your aura.

Regular breath. Continue to clear for one to two minutes.

Exhale.

Pause. In the pause of the exhale, create a clearing vortex on the outside edge of your aura.

From the center of your head, greet your 6th Vortex and any feeling of deadness.

Inhale. Be in your practice, supported by Earth flow, Sky flow and contained by your Breath of Life. Allow the clearing vortex to begin to pull deadness out of your 6th Vortex.

Regular breath. Adjust your practice if you need to.

Know, as it is releasing, the container of your own Breath of Life. Know that the deadness has come from the loss of our own sight. Seeing through someone else's eyes is never the same. Seeing through someone else's soul essence is what creates the deadness.

Allow the clearing vortex to begin to clear information out of your 6th Vortex that is not in affinity with your soul essence knowing.

Regular breath. Clear, for one to two minutes.

Exhale.

Pause. In the pause of the exhale, be with your soul essence sphere in the center of your head and in communication with your still point in the flow of mantle, supported by Earth flow and Sky flow, and awakened to the knowledge of sight and abilities in your 6th Vortex.

Your 6th Vortex is the soul access Vortex – the container of the point of origin of soul essence sphere.

Inhale.

Exhale.

Pause. In the pause of the exhale, connect thumb to pinky finger. Be with the information you have just heard about the 6th Vortex.

Inhale.

Exhale.

On the pause, be with the information regarding the 6th Vortex.

Regular breath. Repeat for three to four breaths. When it has completed, the Vortex will close and the energy will dissipate.

Activating Aspect of the 6th Vortex

Exhale.

Pause. In the pause of the exhale, ask from your soul essence sphere in the center of your head for a quartz crystal seed to be created on the outside edge of your aura.

Supported in your Embodied Practice, ask from the center of your head with your soul essence sphere, for the aspect of the 6th Vortex, the word "catalyst" to appear above the quartz crystal seed.

When you are ready, ask from the center of your head with your soul essence sphere for the word "catalyst" to drop into the crystal seed. It drops into the seed. Ask for it to change to the vibration of your soul aspect that your body is ready to work from.

The seed will change to pure energy vibration. You may sense, see, or know that it is there. It will move into your 6th Vortex

Charging Catalyst in 6th Vortex

Exhale.

Pause. In the pause of the exhale, connect thumb to pinky finger. Be with the energy of catalyst as it enlivens your 6th Vortex.

Inhale. Charge catalyst in your 6th Vortex.

Pause. Hold, in the fullness of breath. Be with the energy of catalyst in your 6th Vortex.

Exhale. Move and sense through the energy of catalyst.

Repeat two to three times

Exhale.

Pause. In the pause of the exhale, allow your soul essence to greet your 6th Vortex.
Inhale.
Pause. In the pause of the exhale, allow your still point in the flow of mantle to greet your 6th Vortex.
The 6th Vortex, the container of soul essence in the body, in communication with all, held by your sacred space in the flow of mantle - so that your soul essence is safe.

Close your practice by following Closing of Practice and Complete Sections in the Supplemental Chapter.

Color of 6th Vortex

Our 6th Vortex point of origin color is yellow. Yellow is the center of frequency and wavelength. This balance in wavelength and frequency provides the soul essence sphere protection from the light that blinds or keeps us in illusion.

A popular color to activate in the 6th is indigo, which has a high frequency and short wavelengths. The soul essence does not have the space in the short wavelengths to hold against other energy and information intruding on its soul essence relay station.

Practice Segment 20 - Color Activation of the 6th Vortex

Note: Wait one to two weeks after Vortex activation before doing this color activation.

Open your Embodied Practice by following the Seated Practice, Soul Essence in the Center of the Head, Grounding, Aural, Four-Part Breath, Earth Flow, and Sky Flow in the Supplemental Chapter.

Exhale.
Pause. In the pause of the exhale, connect thumb to pinky finger.
Through your soul essence sphere in the center of your head, create a clearing vortex on the outside edge of your aura.
Inhale.
Exhale.
Pause. In the pause of the exhale, through your soul essence sphere, greet Earth and ask it to send a stream of energy upward, stopping 19 to 22 inches out in front of you, at nose height.
Inhale.
Exhale.
Pause. Through your soul essence sphere, greet Sky and ask Sky to drop a thin strand of energy downward, to meet a strand of Earth energy.
Regular breath. The two energies will meet and will form the clearing vortex.

Inhale.
From the center of your head, greet your 6th Vortex.
Through your soul essence, ask the clearing vortex to pull whatever is blocking your 6th Vortex from being the container that it needs to hold the vibration and frequency of the point of origin color vibration, yellow.

142

Exhale.
Pause. In the pause of the exhale, continue to allow the clearing vortex to pull energy that is blocking the container of your 6th Vortex.

Regular Breath.

If you feel uncomfortable during this clearing, remember to adjust your Earth and Sky, so that your body is supported in the practice. If you feel anxious, continue to use settling breath, which is on the pause of the exhale, connecting thumb to pinky finger.

Now that we have created the container to hold the functional aspect of catalyst, it is safe to begin to release the strong feelings from our 6th Vortex of what occurred - that this did not happen when you were young, like it was meant to.
The opening of the 6th Vortex occurs when the child or adult feels they are able to protect the soul essence that will start to gather there when activated. The 6th Vortex will not develop or open until the children's experience is that they may stand on their own. This comes from a complex completion of energetic developmental tasks and the 1st, 2nd, and 3rd Vortexes developing.
Begin to allow the clearing vortex to pull the feelings that had you close your 6th Vortex. Remember, you were born seeing energy and your 6th Vortex was working. You may have closed it because you were ready to make the journey to develop your other Vortexes or you may have been in fear and overwhelm; allow yourself permission to release. Remember to stay in the center of your head with your soul essence sphere as you allow the clearing vortex to draw out the feelings why your 6th Vortex closed and why it was or is feeling fearful to open. Do this for two to three minutes. The clearing vortex will close and the energy will dissipate when complete.

Exhale.
Pause. In the pause of the exhale, allow a yellow droplet to form on the outside edge of your aura - the size of a drop of water.
Inhale.
Exhale.
Pause. In the pause of the exhale, connect thumb to pinky. Be with your soul essence in the center of your head. Be with the dot of yellow on outside of your aura.
Inhale when ready, connect thumb to ring finger. Know the experience of seeing through the vibration and frequency of yellow.
Pause. Hold in the fullness of breath. Connect thumb to middle finger. Allow the communication with yellow to be.
Exhale. Connect thumb to pointer. Be in relationship to the frequency of yellow.
Regular breath.
Repeat the Four-Part Breath, two to three times.

Exhale.
Pause. In the pause of the exhale, connect thumb to pinky finger. Through your soul essence sphere, greet the container in the core of your 6th Vortex.
Inhale. Pulsate to meet the core of your 6th Vortex.
Pause. Hold in the fullness of breath, connect thumb to middle finger. Be with the con-

tainer in your 6th Vortex.

Exhale. On the exhale, connect thumb to pointer finger. Invite yellow energy to the exact center where the container formed, to accept the vibration and frequency of yellow into your 6th Vortex.

Regular breath.

Exhale.

Pause. In the pause of the exhale, have permission to see.

Inhale. Take in permission.

Pause. Have permission to see through the interrelatedness of being.

Exhale. Take in permission to see.

Repeat three to four times.

Adjust practice, release down grounding if you need to.

Close your practice by following Closing of Practice and Complete Sections in the Supplemental Chapter.

Chapter 17

Embodied Relationship Halo
The 7th Vortex

The 7th Vortex is the Halo Vortex. It is an Embodied Relationship Vortex and therefore functions inside and outside of the physical body. Its physical point of origin is in the white matter of the brain, specifically the corpus callosum. White matter consists of the connective strains through the brain. From an energetic standpoint, they act as a container for the glia cells to be in communication with the dark matter and dark energy of the solar system and Universe, through pulse field relationship.

Aspects

Brain Works

Our understanding of flow, the aspect of the 7th Vortex, is directly related to our understanding of the part of the brain it occupies, the white matter.

The one that we are most familiar with is the corpus callosum, which connects the right and left hemisphere through the fibrous strands. From there feelers go off to into each hemisphere. The more ordered and even the structure is, the better the brain functions. The organized structure of the white matter also balances the production of neurotransmitters, such as gaba and glutamate, in a balanced fashion.

This is significant if we want to begin to think about how working with our Vortexes can change all aspects of our life. We are awakening to a new understanding that as we work with the 7th Vortex we are also working with the white matter of the brain. The 7th Vortex's job is intercommunication with the right and left hemisphere and then ultimately the downward flow of communication with the central nervous system. The energy uses the central nervous systems' nerves, housed within the spinal column, as its highway. Sky energy runs through this highway to energize and move into the rest of our body.

This is quite an important Vortex since it is interconnected to Sky information. This type of communication is accessed because the 7th Vortex is also out of the body. The communication coming in from the aural field is funneled into the 7th Vortex and helps support the white matter of the brain in terms of its growth, development and modulation of signals within the brain.

The more balanced and even the structure of our white matter is in our brain, the healthier and more balanced we are as human beings. We are healthier from a neural transmitter state and from our ability to learn and triage, or move around information within our brain.

Abilities

Learning To Walk Before We Run

As we understand the structure of the 7th Vortex and the brain, we can begin to open to the understanding of why we first connect to Sky in Embodied Practice.

Like when a child stands and walks too early before the psoas, leg and buttock muscles are ready, they often have trouble with lower back, hips and knees in adolescence or mid-life. This is also true when we use our 7th Vortex. We need to open to Sky so our corpus callosum can develop in balance. Why do the four layers of atmosphere develop our corpus callosum? To answer, the four winds in many cultures and religions had wonderful significance. Ultimately they keep our atmosphere (our weather on Earth) in relative balance, in terms of seasons and what different species need that occupy different parts of Earth. The wind patterns enable our Earth's atmosphere to be balanced.

Recall the layers of the atmosphere we connect to. The first layer, the troposphere, is where the winds are. The south wind is the nurturing warmth of the day. The east winds are the refreshing and renewing energy. The north wind is the quickening; it makes things happen. The west wind is the warm, wet, and it supports us in our retreat within or our settling. Connecting with this layer of sky aids the corpus callosum in balancing. Once we connect to the atmosphere, we can mirror in our brains, the way in which the flow of the four winds balance energy in the system.

The next layer in the atmosphere that comes into communication with our 7th Vortex is the stratosphere. This is where the ozone layer is functioning for us. Basically, ozone is created by a transfer of atoms. When O_2 atoms are combined, O_3 (ozone) is created. As we come into communication with this (not that we communicate with the ozone), we are communicating from our 7th Vortex with that aspect. The aspect of the ozone layer teaches our white matter about how the transfer of molecules works and the function of that process, because the ozone layer protects us. This awakens neural protection portions in the corpus callosum.

Then we have the mesosphere. This is where a lot of debris burns up. Many meteors never make it to Earth because they burn up in this part of the atmosphere. This layer has a very high temperature. Communication with the mesosphere gives our brain the structure and understanding of the function of heat transformation, to put it in simple terms. It is a lot more complicated than that, but this is a good building block of information.

The thermosphere, which is the outermost layer, is very thin and has extremely cold temperatures. Here is where we begin to learn to communicate with our 7th Vortex to energies of the solar system. Once we have learned to communicate comfortably from our white matter and our 7th Vortex with that intense energy of the thermosphere, then over time we become ready to move on to communicate with the solar system.

Learning about the white matter of the brain goes far beyond these simple basic body processes. Even at this early stage of Embodied Practice, the learning and developing of the white matter, emerging from its contact with Sky, is beyond profound. It can take years of Embodied Practice.

Function

About 40% of the brain consists of white matter, which contains fibers called neurons that transmit pulses in the brain. The remainder is gray matter. The white matter is the avenue of communication between multiple gray matter sections and between gray matter and other parts of the body's central nervous system. Think of the gray matter as a computer's CPU, and think of white matter as the circuit board through which the CPU does its work by connecting it with other parts.

Without <u>healthy</u> white matter, the brain cannot function in a proper manner. White matter disease occurs when lesions appear in the white matter.

As much as the structure inside of this white matter resembles a lacey round structure, when looked at, the 7th Vortex's energy looks like a halo. You may have seen this in pictures. It is the energy outside the body that looks like a halo.

Each of the Vortexes meet. The white matter comes down to the top of the 6th Vortex. The physical structures of the 6th and 7th Vortexes meet at the white matter at the top of the third ventricle and thalamus, which is the point of origin of the 6th Vortex. This white matter then comes around the 6th Vortex and moves down the spinal column and down the central nervous system. This is the association with our back channels. Each Vortex is connected to the back channel. It is through this flow in the back channels and through the central nervous system that the energy we bring in through the 7th Vortex is able to have direct communication to each of the Vortexes, a beautiful dance of Reflective Relationship.

Practice Segment 21 - Activation of Halo - The 7th Vortex

Open your Embodied Practice by following the Seated Practice, Soul Essence in Center of Head, Grounding, Aural, Four-Part Breath, Earth Flow, and Sky Flow from the Supplemental Chapter.

Point of Origin Clearing of Flow in the 7th Vortex

Exhale.
Pause. Through your soul essence sphere in the center of your head, ask to create a clearing vortex on the outside edge of your aura.
Inhale.
Exhale.
Pause. In the pause of the exhale, through your soul essence sphere, greet Earth and ask it to send a stream of energy upward, stopping 19 to 22 inches out in front of you, at nose height.
Inhale.

Exhale.

Pause. Through your soul essence sphere, greet Sky and ask Sky to drop a thin strand of energy downward, to meet a strand of Earth energy.

Regular breath. The two energies will meet and will form the clearing vortex.

From the center of your head and with your soul essence sphere, greet your 7th Embodied Relationship Vortex. Your 7th Vortex is located at the top of your head, radiating upwards in an expanding cone.

Inhale.

Exhale.

Pause. In the pause of the breath, connect thumb to pinky finger. Be with your 7th Vortex.

Allow your breath to continue. Inhale when you need to and, in every pause, be with your 7th Vortex.

Take three to four breaths. Be with your 7th Vortex.

Clear Flow

Exhale.

Pause.

From the center of your head with your soul essence sphere, greet the clearing vortex you created on the outside edge of your aura.

Inhale.

Begin to release anything in the 7th Vortex that blocks it from communicating with flow. It is not important that you understand what flow or being in communication with the flow means - you will learn that through coming into communication with flow through your emergence into the body. The aspect creates the space for the Vortex to begin to form.

Regular breath.

Focus, in the pause of the breath, and allow the clearing vortex to do its work. Attract and draw, from your 7th Vortex, what is not in alignment with flow in the 7th Vortex. During the clearing, if you feel uncomfortable, adjust your Earth and Sky flow. Remember that you can release feelings or uncomfortable body feelings down your grounding corridor into Earth, whenever you need to. Do this for one to two minutes. The clearing vortex will close and the energy will dissipate, when ready.

Exhale.

Pause. In the pause of the exhale, connect thumb to pinky finger.

From the center of your head, create a clearing vortex on the outside edge of your aura. **Allow** the clearing vortex to continue to do its work and continue to clear lack of connection to flow.

Clear Confusion

Exhale.

Pause. In the pause of the exhale, connect thumb to pinky finger.

From the center of your head, greet your 7th Vortex and the clearing vortex. Know that a deep confusion may be coming up about what the cognitive brain missed, to not make true sense out of life. Self-defeat, overwhelm with disorganization, confusion about reality, what is real, and lack of affinity with position in life. Allow whatever comes up to be pulled into the clearing vortex on the outside edge of your aura.

Take five or six breaths, clearing confusion.

The clearing vortex will close and the energy will dissipate, when complete.

Clear Loss or Fear of Abyss

Exhale.

Pause. In the pause of the exhale, through your soul essence sphere, greet Earth and ask it to send a stream of energy upward, stopping 19 to 22 inches out in front of you, at nose height.

Inhale.

Exhale.

Pause. Through your soul essence sphere, greet Sky and ask Sky to drop a thin strand of energy downward, to meet a strand of Earth energy.

Regular breath. The two energies will meet and will form the clearing vortex.

Inhale.

Exhale.

Pause. In the pause of the exhale, create a clearing vortex on the outside edge of your aura. From the center of your head, greet your 7th Vortex and the feeling of loss.

Regular breath.

Be in your practice, supported by Earth flow, Sky flow, and contained by your Breath of Life. Allow the clearing vortex to begin to pull loss or the fear of the abyss out of your 7th Vortex.

Adjust your practice if you need to.

Know, as it is releasing and as you are supported by Earth flow, Sky flow and the container of your own Breath of Life, that the loss or fear of the abyss has come from not being taught how to communicate through flow. Most of us were rejected, punished, left alone, or diagnosed if we tried to explore the flow relationship with the electromagnetic field of Sky, or schooled into fear because it did not fit a specific religious dogma.

Allow it to begin to clear information out of your 7th Vortex that is not in affinity with your ability to communicate with flow.

Continue to clear lack of affinity for three or four breaths.

Be with your soul essence sphere in the center of your head and in communication with your still point in the flow of mantle, supported by Earth flow and Sky flow, awakened to the knowledge of flow relationship and the abilities of your 7th Vortex.

Your 7th Vortex is the top point of the physical Vortex column. It is the physical aspect of the flow of Sky or Earth's container. Your 7th Vortex access communicates through the white matter in the brain, which communicates as one system - with origins of the whole, of left and right hemispheres, which (through the corpus callosum) connect the cortex to the mid-brain stem (back channels), flow and communication in the body.

Exhale.

Pause. In the pause of the exhale, connect thumb to pinky finger. Be with the information you have just heard about the 7th Vortex.

Inhale.

Exhale.

Pause. In the pause of the exhale, be with the information regarding the 7th Vortex.
Regular breath. Continue to clear for two to three breaths.
When complete, the clearing vortex will close and the energy will dissipate.

Put in Communication with Soul Essence and Sacred Space

Quartz Crystal Seed

Exhale.
Pause. In the pause of the exhale, ask from your soul essence sphere in the center of your head for a quartz crystal seed to be created on the outside edge of your aura.
Inhale.
Supported in your Embodied Practice and from the center of your head with your soul essence sphere, ask for the aspect of the 7th Vortex, "flow," to appear above the quartz crystal seed.
Regular breath.
When you are ready, ask from the center of your head for the word "flow" to drop into the crystal seed. As it drops into the seed, ask for it to change to the vibration of your soul aspect that your body is ready to work from.
The crystal seed will change to pure energy vibration. You may sense, see, or know that it is there. It will move into your 7th Vortex when ready.
Regular breath for three to six breaths.

Charging Flow in 7th Vortex

Exhale.
Pause. In the pause of the exhale, connect thumb to pinky finger. Be with the energy of flow in your 7th Vortex.
Inhale. Charge flow in your 7th Vortex.
Pause. In the fullness of breath, be with flow in your 7th Vortex.
Exhale. Move and sense through the energy of flow.
Repeat this Four-Part Breath four to six times.

7th Vortex Greets Sacred Space in Flow of Mantle

Exhale.
Pause. In the pause of the exhale, allow your soul essence to greet your 7th Vortex.
Inhale.
Exhale.
Pause. In the pause of the exhale, allow your still point in the flow of mantle to greet your 7th Vortex.
The 7th Vortex, the top position of the Vortex column, the vehicle of orientation to Sky - allow the white matter to know.
On the next pause of exhale, have your 1st Vortex greet your still point in the flow of mantle.
On your next pause of exhale, have your 1st Vortex greet your 2nd Vortex.
On your next pause of exhale, have your 2nd Vortex greet your 3rd Vortex.
On your next pause of exhale, have your 3rd Vortex greet your 4th Vortex.

On your next pause of exhale, have your 4th Vortex greet your 5th Vortex.
On your next pause of exhale, have your 5th Vortex greet your 6th Vortex.
On your next pause of exhale, have your 6th Vortex greet your 7th Vortex.
Regular breath.
Take three or four breaths until you feel complete with all Vortexes come into communication.

Close your practice by following Closing of Practice and Complete Sections in the Supplemental Chapter.

Color of 7th Vortex

The 7th Halo Vortex color point of origin color activation is red-violet. It has a low frequency and longer wavelengths. Red-violet aids us in modulating energy from out of the body into the body. The 8th Vortex, the Wheel Vortex, which resides solely in the aura, is the Vortex that takes everything in from cosmic flow and sorts it. We learn about developing the 8th Vortex in Pulse Practice. The 7th Vortex chooses and allows what is in communication with soul essence to come into the soul body.

The popular color used with the 7th Vortex is violet, which has a high frequency and short wavelengths. Violet has short wavelengths which don't allow for the entering energy to be modulated. This lack of modulation overwhelms the corpus callosum and the soul essence does not know it is safe to come into communication with the soul body – resulting in an induced brain state which occurs prior to brain death. This is the same as a drugged brain. This may result long term in a loss of our neural ability to be fully in the body. Being fully in the body is the only mechanism organizing our body's systems to come out of the abyss.

Practice Segment 22 - Color Activation of the 7th Vortex

Note: Wait one to two weeks after 7th Vortex activation before doing color activation.

Open your Embodied Practice by following the Seated Practice, Soul Essence in the Center of the Head, Grounding, Aural, Four-Part Breath, Earth Flow, and Sky Flow in the Supplemental Chapter.

From the center of your head with your soul essence sphere, greet your 7th Vortex.
Inhale. Ask your soul essence sphere to create a clearing vortex.
Exhale.
Pause. In the pause of the exhale, through your soul essence sphere, greet Earth and ask it to send a stream of energy upward, stopping 19 to 22 inches out in front of you, at nose height.
Inhale.
Exhale.
Pause. Through your soul essence sphere, greet Sky and ask Sky to drop a thin strand of energy downward to meet a strand of Earth energy.
Regular breath. The two energies will meet and will form the clearing vortex.

Through your soul essence, ask the clearing vortex to pull whatever is blocking your 7th Vortex from being the container that it needs to hold the vibration and frequency of the original color vibration.

Exhale.

Pause. In the pause of the exhale, continue to allow the clearing vortex to pull the energy that is blocking the container of your 7th Vortex.

Regular Breath.

If you feel uncomfortable during this clearing, remember to adjust your Earth and Sky, so that your body is supported in the practice. If you feel anxious, continue to use your Settling Breath, connecting thumb to pinky finger on the pause of the exhale.

Regular breath. Take two to three breaths.

Now that we have created the container to hold the functional aspect of flow, which is vibration and frequency, it is safe to begin to release the strong feelings from our 7th Vortex of what occurred - that this did not happen when you were young, like it was meant to.

Exhale.

Pause. Give yourself two to three breaths while reading below.

This contact is what creates the container and the 7th Vortex to hold the vibration of communication with Sky. The soul takes measures of protection if the 7th Vortex doesn't have its modulating functions, deems energetic development unsafe, and begins to look outside of self for safety.

Exhale.

Pause. In the pause of the exhale, release what was hooked up to your 7th Vortex (out of desperation for guidance) into the clearing vortex. Release what happened as your soul moved out in inspiration and was stopped, or as you looked for inspiration and none could be found. Remember to stay in the center of your head with your soul essence sphere.

Regular breath. Taking two to six breaths clearing what was hooked up.

When complete for today, the Vortex will close and the energy will dissipate.

Exhale.

Pause. In the pause of the exhale, allow a red-violet droplet to form on the outside edge of your aura - the size of a drop of water.

Inhale.

Exhale. In the pause of the exhale, connect thumb to pinky finger. Be with your soul essence sphere in the center of your head. Be with the dot of red-violet on outside of your aura.

Pause.

Inhale when ready. Connect thumb to ring finger. Know the properties of being in communication, or taking in communication, through the vibration and frequency of red-violet.

Pause. In the fullness of breath, connect thumb to middle finger. Allow the inspiration through red-violet to be.

Exhale, in relationship to the frequency of red-violet.

Repeat the Four-Part Breath two to three times.

Exhale. In the pause of the exhale, connect thumb to pinky finger. Through your soul essence sphere, greet the container in the core of your 7th Vortex.

Inhale. Pulsate upward to meet the core of your 7th Vortex.

Pause. In the fullness of breath, connect thumb to middle finger. Be with the container in your 7th Vortex.

Exhale. In the exhale, connect thumb to pointer finger. Invite the red violet energy to the exact center where the container formed, to accept the vibration and frequency of red-violet.

Repeat the Four-Part Breath pattern two to three times.

Exhale.

Pause. In the pause of the exhale, connect thumb to pinky finger. Think of one thing you would like to communicate with Sky about. It could be an aspect of your life. It could be an aspect of past, future, anything that you would like to be in communication about. It could be something that you would like to tell Sky or something that you would like to ask.

Inhale.

Exhale.

Pause. In the pause of the exhale, be in communication through red violet frequency and vibration with whatever you would like to communicate with Sky. Give yourself permission in the center of your head to know that the communication is occurring.

Regular breath.

Close your practice by following Closing of Practice and Complete Sections in the Supplemental Chapter.

Embodied Relationship Vortexes

Vortex	Name	Location	Element	Aspect	Abilities
1	**Flow/Form Vortex** Violet	Sacrum, Top of Coccyx	Water	Biological Essence	Communication through water. Connection to flow. Vestibular intuition.
7	**Halo Vortex** Light that blinds Red-Violet	Top of head.	Dark energy	Flow	Communication through bringing energy from other realms into a form the body can use. Transfer energy.
Hand Right	**Hand Vortex**	Center of palm.		Possibility	Ability to effect change.
Hand Left	**Hand Vortex**	Center of palm.		Possibility	Ability to effect change.
Foot Right	**Foot Vortex**	Center bottom of foot.		Being with	Ability to walk your path.
Foot Left	**Foot Vortex**	Center bottom of foot.		Being with	Ability to walk your path.

Note: Human Relationship Embodied Vortexes normally operate for daily functions in and out of the physical body.

Embodied Vortexes

Through Embodied Practice, our energetic structures develop giving use to the field functions of the Vortexes in our body.

Vortex	Name	Location	Element	Aspect	Commonly Known Abilities
2	**Sensing Vortex** Blue.	4th and 5th Lumbar vertebrae.	Earth	Sensing	Field-to-field transfer. Chi charging and flow. Original seed.
3	**Body Relationship Vortex** Green.	Thoracic 12 to Lumbar 1.	Air, wood	Pulse Fields Earth & Sky Field Transfer	Energetically supports kinesis cell signaling, the balance of Sky (yang) and Earth (yin), the signaling of what is offered Initiating charging point of the Breath of Life. Energetically support peptide digestion. Signals body to turn gene expression, protein synthesis, and neural modulation on/off. Connection to energetic sleep-body. Information processing from energetic sleep-body. The body's ability to make appropriate sense out of what occurred or was experienced in dream fields, and which ones you were in.
4	**Field Sphere** Red.	Thoracic 6 and 7	Photon Light	Field Generator	Affinity with self and others. The structure of soul essence line.
5	**Unseen Vortex** Orange.	Between C7 and T1	Fire	Space between vibration	Clairaudience. Hearing Vibratory words. Inner voice. Knowledge from the spaces-in-between in the body. Whisper of the Soul. Connection to human field.
6	**Soul Essence Access Vortex** Gold.	3rd Ventricle	Metal	Catalyst	Clairvoyance. Abstract intuition. Transfer energy.

Note: Human Embodied Vortexes normally operate for daily functions, only inside the physical body.

Chapter 18

Dance of Reflective Relationship

As we have completed Embodied Practice segments throughout this book, we begin to move back into our position in reflective relationship between Earth and Sky. For this to happen, the correct mechanisms must be present to transfer information or energy from one place to another. Without these mechanisms, we stay in the abyss and cannot find our way back to soul essence communication. Our soul essence (organized photon light) communicates with our chromosomes to create our soul body. This ignites energy transfer via our soul essence through our vibratory bioelectric human body. The Dance of Reflective Relationship!

The experience of our soul essence moving through our vibratory bioelectric soul body is incredible, especially compared to what our soul essence experiences when it's in light form. Our human form experience is worth the hazardous journey; the journey of going into the abyss, of losing the mechanisms of direct communication to our soul essence while we develop the mechanisms in the human form to reconnect to soul essence, and everything else we were in communication with as soul essence, from the pulse fields of the Universe.

When the human field was created, it made our journey through the abyss almost impossible. Yet, our essence still chooses to create a body to try again and again to make it through the abyss into connection through reflective relationship. When the essence creates another soul-body to come through the abyss and to once again establish soul essence connection through soul-body, because of the human field, the 13 Energetic Developmental Stages of Humans still eludes the soul-body. Therefore, without soul orientation, a tremendous loss and sense of overwhelm is created.

Despair of the Dance

We stay lost in the abyss, while in our overwhelmed state, because our biological systems are bound without their energetic connections and cannot be in communication. When we do not understand or know where we are, the brain will make things up. If the prefrontal lobe cannot identify the pictures of the holographic screen of life, it puts itself into an aggravated state. The prefrontal lobe then will make something up to fill in the blanks or tell us where we are, even if it has no idea. This is because our biological system can't survive or thrive in an agitated state. So we make up directions or take directions from anyone to find our way out of the abyss - or we believe that we are talking to wise or powerful energy sources, yet we do not have the orientation to know what or who we are talking to.

Why do we still come?

Due to the splitting of the soul essence from organized photon light as it whispers into the chromosomes so that they line up, through beginning the transfer journey, if the transfer is not interfered with (from the human field), our energetic development would take 15 to 21 years. In a photon light vibration level, this is a blip - so we don't consider that we may get lost and not develop the mechanism of connections. Although, when we are on a vibrational bioelectric level, 15 to 21 years is a long time and we are completely vulnerable to the human field. Once one of us loses our way in the abyss of transformation, it is harder for those who follow to not get lost, because of the mirroring of the relationship of development. Since most of us end up taking directions from someone who is also lost in the abyss, the directions we take walk us deeper into the human field labyrinths.

Soul orientation, via our Embodied mechanisms - soul essence sphere, grounding, position between Earth and Sky, Breath of Life, and activated vortexes – is critical in finding our way through the abyss. Soul orientation gives us the ability to sense who and where we are, even in the abyss, and to know for ourselves which direction to take. These Embodied mechanisms not only provide us with orientation so we can walk our journey to soul essence gathering, but keep us safe.

As you now begin to Dance of Reflective Relationship, be mindful of the Breath of Life, of your charging of the Breath of Life, of your cobalt blue outside line of your aura, and of your Breath of Life container aiding your soul essence to be safe. The Dance in Reflective Relationship is lost if the soul essence is not safe to come into communication with the soul-body. During the years of developing your mechanisms, it is important to be in contact with an Embodied Practice teacher, ever mindful of the Embodied Principles to keep your soul essence safe.

Gathering of Inner Light

The gathering of inner light is the mechanism of rejoining all of our souls that our soul essence has created. We are awakening to the knowing that the soul essence creates the soul as the body and develops each soul through life experiences.

These soul past-life footprints are gathered in each incarnation. When our energy leaves the biological body (because it will not house the soul energy that has been brought in), it leaves an energetic footprint of the vortexes in the human electromagnetic field. Our past life footprints are like the trail of breadcrumbs Hansel and Gretel dropped in the woods to find their way back home through the dark woods. The footprints are mechanisms of completeness and for if something goes wrong on the transition journey through the abyss of 15 to 21 years (or longer). Everything we learned and experienced is coded and, on death, released in light form.

Once Embodied Basic Practice is mastered, we are able to begin to heal and organize our past life footprints. This allows us to have our footprints take their rightful place within the vortex column, between Earth and Sky in our current life. It takes between one and five years to integrate each past-life footprint into our current vortex structure. During that time, we master everything that was learned or mastered in that past life. Each time, it brings us to a completion beyond words, furthering and deepening our soul orientation and our ability to see across time and space, connecting to everything.

Holographic Universe
(Soul Lens)

To understand Soul Lens, we must first have a basic understanding of how our holographic universe works.

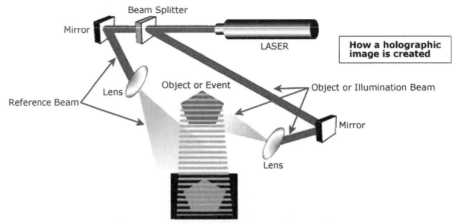

Film (looks like disorganized particles until illuminated by reference beam

Further reading: *The Holographic Universe* by Michael Talbot

Embodied Understanding of the Holographic Universe and the Gathering of Inner Light

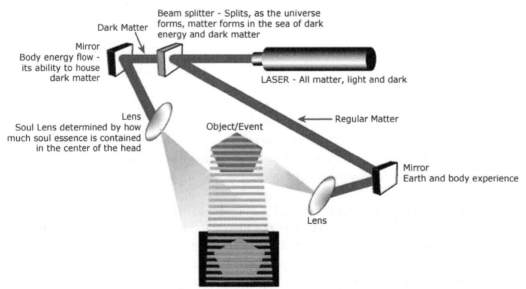

Film - What is higher consciousness?

Soul Orientation Dance of Perception

The gathering of inner light gives us our soul essence lens. Our soul essence lens, or the ability to house our soul essence energy in our third ventricle, directly affects our use and function of our prefrontal lobes. When our prefrontal lobes evolved, they were never meant to function without our soul essence lens.

The field of quantum physics has given us part of the understanding of how we have a vibratory bioelectric experience through the holographic nature of the Universe. Since it is through this holographic nature that we live, it is important to understand how holograms work.

In the diagram of the hologram, there is the source of laser light. The light must pass through a splitter, becoming two beams of light. Each stream of light is reflected off a mirror and focused through a lens. The beam on the right side of the diagram reflects only a scattering of light from the image, so when the beam on the right side of the diagram displays its holographic image, it is only one of disorganized light. The image is unrecognizable. When the reference beam from the left side of the diagram projects onto the holographic image of scattered light, the scattered light organizes and we can clearly see what the holographic image is.

Our reference beam determines what we are experiencing or viewing as the holographic image, which is our life experience. When we do not come into soul orientation, our soul essence cannot take its rightful place as the reference beam, enabling us to see the truth of the scattered light images of life experience. When other things are used as reference beams, we end up living in the distortion of the human field, never really knowing what we are seeing or experiencing, lost in the abyss.

Soul Essence Lens

Elaborating on our holographic experience through our Principles of Embodiment, the source of light (our soul essence) goes through a split. Our soul essence splits off when it communicates with the chromosomes and begins its journey into human soul form, after which, we have many more than two mirrors we reflect from. This is determined in our mirrored nature of being. Reflected through the mirrors of life, a scattered light image appears (the confusion of life) on the center space of the diagram. A reference beam is needed for the scattered light to organize into a picture or cohesive experience. Here we can stay lost in the abyss, ever letting our prefrontal lobes be the reference beam, telling us what the scattered light looks like. Our soul essence lens, in our third ventricle, which comes as an end result of energetic development or embodiment, holds the key to being able to organize the scattered light into soul orientation and dancing in Reflective Relationship between Earth and Sky.

We hold a sacred awakening that without our soul essence lens which forms from completing the 13 Energetic Developmental Stages of Humans, Embodied Practice, and the gathering of our past life footprints, we perceive only disorganized light. Our brains then begin making up what they are looking at and make up an explanation or association. If they do not, the hypothalamus-pituitary-axis stays over excited – which excessively stimulates our stress responses. This becomes a physical survival issue that must be satisfied. So, we have all been living in the confusion of scattered light in the abyss, lost, and always seeking the reconnection to our soul essence so we can know what the light image is before us, or seeking to discern the truth from the lie.

Simple Example of Essence Sight

I have incarnated through thousands of years, ever taking lives, organizing and coding what humans were before the human field and before we began to lose our connection to our energetically developed way of being.

Our alignment on December 21, 2012, opened a rift in the abyss, giving all of us the chance to reawaken to our energetic nature through soul orientation, dancing in Reflective Relationship, and to be connected across time and space through the embodied vortex that the Earth sits in.

This sets the stage for our understanding that perception is partly determined from what lens we look through and our attachment to a body of knowledge that organizes what we see and what we do.

Have permission to gather your soul essence lens and see the complete picture, the true structure of the light particles on the holographic film of the Universe. Know I am with you and support your essence as you move into Soul Orientation with the Dance of Reflective Relationship.

When you are ready to deepen your Embodied connection, the 13 Energetic Developmental Stages of Humans are available as daily-guided meditations on www.SoulOrientation.com. It is always best to follow Embodied Practice for six months to a year, and receive one to two Embodied healing sessions prior to beginning the first energetic developmental stage, Journey into Form: Soul Self Entry.

The Ocean in me reflects in the Sky in you and the Ocean in you reflects in the Sky in me. I am ever with you, dancing in Reflective Relationship.

The 13 Energetic Developmental Stages of Humans

The 13 Energetic Developmental Stages of Humans came from moon sign, sun sign, and the flux fields. They came, not to meet us with a cognitive knowing, but as poetry, calling us, rocking us, bathing us in the light of the moon, to once again lead us through the abyss to connection with our soul essence.

I brought them to us from dancing and singing, from the stars, so that all could benefit when ready. I recorded and forged the developmental awakening songs into 13 Lunar Cycle Labyrinths which, when walked to the center, the linear labyrinth structure is transcended, thus beginning to move us into pulse relationship as our vortexes develop, enabling a deeper and deeper communication with soul essence.

If you feel called to awaken to our energetic development, begin the Stages and complete them in sequence, 01 to 13.

Awaken 01: Journey into Form: Soul Self-Entry

We pass through two stars that appear one. This journey is the point of origin of being and energetic being, versus a psychological, biological being. No one can teach us or tell us this difference - it must be experienced to have this awaken in us. The passing through is the beginning point of form. When the soul claims the form, we begin our energetic development and lay the groundwork for being in communication with the Universe, versus with human information which has not passed through, but has come from being blinded by light.

If your soul knows somewhere that you are an energetic being with the ultimate capacity to communicate through the human form, walk the labyrinth of soul self entry.

Awaken 02: Taking Form and Being Met

In the 20 years that I have been using my understanding of Being Met, it has been the most difficult for my clients to understand and identify when they have energetically experienced this. The overwhelmed feelings and grief is so great that support is needed to stay and receive the healing. We strongly recommend that this Being Met Awakened Labyrinth be walked on a current emotional issue or topic in your life that you want to create change in. This, then, facilitates the first experience of Being Met in a visible way, which is needed to move into deeper levels of being met.

Being Met determines the energetic core that the personality forms around. It also ultimately determines our ability to self-reference.

Awaken 03: Living in Interrelated Energetic Boundaries

The excitement of this 3rd Awakened Labyrinth (like life) is similar to how we feel at the beginning of a carnival ride. We are so excited for the experience and where the energy will take us. However, if we are too big or too small for the safety harness, we will not be held in place. The ride will gradually overwhelm us, throwing us around. We then become the effect of the energy, instead of experiencing the energy. This Labyrinth provides daily containers and aids our vortexes, as they develop to manage intense energy. Walk this labyrinth and have the experience of living in a container.

Awaken 04: Alignment of 3 in Reflective Movement
Awaken to how movement - in aspect 3 - pushes us in the position of flow. Walking this labyrinth enlivens us in our ability to keep in synch with the changing angles of association, which cascade across the Earth daily. The power of adding reflective movement to your abilities to create in your life must be experienced. This 4th Awakened Labyrinth is also beyond words, when it is walked on a topic or issue.

Awaken 05: Seeds of Passion and Position
This 5th Awakened Labyrinth allows for the awakening of our heart's desire, as an ever-flowing, deeper and deeper connection to what is - our desire flows from this connection and fuels the connection. The underlying principle in this Labyrinth is our ability to transform to obtain our heart's desire. Walk and sow the seeds of passion.

Awaken 06: Reflective Relationship
We enter the 6th Awakened Labyrinth cradling our heart's desire. Cradling brings energy in deeper to open up to the reflective pools in us. This allows us to walk and heal what blocks us from experiencing reflective relationship. As we walk, we learn to bring forward the three aspects of association into our reflective relationship. Our ability to come into reflective relationship sets us free from the burden for the need to forgive – forgiving someone dictates that we must change something that has wounded us into something positive. This is an energetic burden and is not the order of reflective relationship. In reflective relationship, we take in the three angles of association and then reflect them back, as we come into complete relationship with whatever is, without any change to our soul essence. Walk the Labyrinth of Reflective Relationship.

Awaken 07: Being - The Soul Solidarity

The 7th Awakened Labyrinth is one stage that must be mastered or our soul is ever at risk of being led astray. Like the 7th Vortex, this 7th stage is most vulnerable to energetic information that would bind us to something other than soul essence. Humans first bonded to the northern sky, which (for 10,000 years) has made us vulnerable to the loss of our soul solidarity. Walk and claim your connection through soul essence, not some guru, religious philosophy, or popular fad, like drugs, because most don't know or understand the path to energetic being without manipulating the energy.

Awaken 08: Soul Pulse, Inner Fire

This labyrinth, like the 8th Vortex, is one of the entry points into the human vortex system. The 8th Vortex filters and takes in information on a photon-light level, where the energy begins the journey into the body. The energy in the human field, placed here by humans, distorts the energy as it is moves into the 8th Vortex. This distortion stops the gathering of inner light and the soul essence from moving deep into the body vortexes - to aid us in creating change through a deep soul attachment. Leo's flame, in which you will walk, will become the nurturing inner flame in the overwhelming waters of emotion.

We cannot create in flow if we are overtaken by emotion. Walk and gain a core place of holding onto the self, to the soul - in the storm of emotions and the energy of others.

Awaken 09: Meeting the Human Field

The 9th Awakened Labyrinth awakens us to one of the most powerful reasons that souls take form in the body, which is to have the experience of life or deep feelings. For many, feelings have become something that tortures. Walking this labyrinth will provide the mechanism of inner connection, to enable a complete deep experience of all feelings. We call this "Mastery of Emotions." It is the ability to have emotions and feelings, while maintaining a deep connection to all. From this, true purpose emerges.

Awaken 10: Earth Journey: Containing and Using Inner Fire

The 10th Awakened Labyrinth's first corner is "Body Energy States." This dictates that the Awakened Labyrinth is about our ability to maintain our own energetic boundaries - relating to our relationship to self, Earth, and the pull of the closest spiral galaxies. Developmentally, this represents our ability to use our inner fire and contain it by utilizing our ability of reflective relationship. Then, we are able to resist the urge to merge energetically, which is one of the points of origin of the cause of the loss of communication with our soul essence.

Walk and learn to be comfortable in your own energetic sphere of being and never experience loneliness again.

Awaken 11: Being the Bridge between Earth and Sky

As we enter the 11th Labyrinth, with moon sign and sun sign in Libra, we call on three interconnecting triangles. These triangles appear as we connect the stars. We enter this labyrinth adjacent to the body energy corner. In walking this labyrinth, we find our stance and we become the bridge between Earth and Sky. Walk and experience being the bridge between Earth and Sky to begin an awareness of why humanity resides on land.

Awaken 12: Creating With the Raw Energy of the Universe

We walk this 12th Awakened Labyrinth to learn to contain the raw energy of creation. This is the underpinning to see the truth from a lie and to contain the ability to see the creation energy behind something. This lets us see if lies were created whole or pieced together to deceive. We enter the labyrinth with moon sign in Scorpio and sun sign in Scorpio. We are walking to get free of its sting; that which numbed us against our desire to learn to contain the raw energy of creation.

Awaken 13: The Journey of One Becoming Two, and Two Becoming One

The journey of one becoming two is the most powerful - in terms of our energetic development, because if one never became two, there would be no Universe or life as we experience it. We walk to experience our soul being one, then becoming two, then becoming one again. As we develop the container of the heart and two becomes one again, we integrate our past life footprints.

Chapter 19

Supplemental

Note: These practice segments are to be used to open vortex aspect and color activation, or in a daily Embodied Practice.

Seated Practice, Coming into Position

Sit supported and relaxed in your chair, legs at a right angle, knees level with hips. Arms relaxed on your lap, your hands up. Place your shoulders where they feel most relaxed. Rest your head in a neutral position.

Note: Seated Practice is a powerful soul self-position practice that can be used in any life circumstance to gain functional support of ourselves.

Soul Essence in the Center of the Head

Exhale.
Pause. On the pause of the exhale, connect thumb to pinky.
Inhale when you are ready.
Exhale.
Pause. On the pause of the exhale, connect thumb to pinky. In that pause, be with your soul essence pulse in the aural center of your head or physical center of head.
Inhale when needed.
Regular breath. Continue and be with your soul essence sphere.
Exhale. On the pause of the exhale, connect thumb to pinky. Be with your soul essence sphere.
Inhale. Soul essence sphere in the aural center of your head pulsates out to the size of a large marble.
Exhale. On the pause of the exhale, connect thumb to pinky. Still in the pause, greet the soul essence sphere in the aural center of your head.
Inhale when you need to. As you inhale, continue to allow your soul essence sphere to expand to the size of a large marble.
Exhale. Allow your soul essence sphere to slowly pulsate in like a heartbeat.
Pause. Connect thumb to pinky finger. Be with your soul essence sphere in the aural center of your head. Imagine snuggling into this safe space in the aural center of your head.
Inhale when you need to. Soul essence sphere pulsates like a heartbeat out to meet.
Take two to three breaths and repeat. Allow yourself to be nurtured by your soul essence.

Center of the Head Practice

Inhale. Soul essence sphere in the center of your head pulses out to meet.
Exhale.
Inhale. Soul essence sphere continues to expand out till it reaches the size of a large marble.
Exhale. Soul essence sphere pulses in like a heartbeat.
Inhale. Soul essence sphere pulses out to meet.
Exhale. Soul essence sphere pulses in gathering its soul essence energy.
Inhale. Soul essence sphere pulses out to meet.
Continue soul essence pulse breath as long as you need to connect to your soul essence pulse in the center of your head.

Grounding

Exhale.
Pause. In the pause of the exhale, greet your four aspects of grounding. First greet the aspect of the feminine on the left side.
Regular breath. As you greet the aspect of the feminine, be aware if it is in communication or out of communication. Ask through the center of your head, your soul essence sphere, for it to be in communication. If you are out of communication, take time to clear it with a dot of gold.
Exhale. On the pause of the exhale, say 'hello' to the grounding aspect of the masculine on the right side of your grounding disc. Ask for it to be in communication.
Regular breath.
Exhale.
Pause. On the pause of the exhale, greet the aspect of the finite, which is the back position of the grounding disc, asking it to be in communication. If you are out of communication, take time to clear it with a dot of gold.
Regular breath.
Exhale.
Pause. On the pause of the exhale, greet the aspect of the infinite, which is the front position of the grounding disc, asking it to be in communication. If you are out of communication, take time to clear it with a dot of gold.
Inhale.
Exhale when ready.
Have your grounding corridor pulsate down in communication with your still point in the flow of mantle.
Exhale.

Aural

Inhale. On the inhale, breathe into the sternum, opening.
Exhale. Let the sternum relax down and a little bit back.
Inhale. Sternum opens.

Exhale. Sternum relaxes down and back.

Continue these focused sternum breaths for three to four minutes or until you feel contained in your own electromagnetic field of your heart.

Four-Part Breath

Exhale.

Pause. On the pause of the exhale, connect thumb to pinky finger. Allow your body to begin to settle into the practice.

Inhale. Connect thumb to ring finger.

Pause. In the fullness of breath, connect thumb to middle finger.

Exhale. Connect thumb to pointer finger.

Pause. On the pause, connect thumb to pinky finger, settling.

Inhale. Connect thumb to ring finger.

Pause. In the fullness of breath, connect thumb to middle finger.

Exhale. Connect thumb to pointer finger.

Pause.

(Continue Four-Part Breath for two to three minutes).

Earth Flow

Exhale.

Inhale. Soul essence pulse pulsates out like a heartbeat and Earth flow pulses on the outside of your grounding corridor up to charge the perineum.

Exhale.

Pause. In the pause of the exhale, through your soul essence sphere, greet your feet vortexes and ask them to pulse open to just the right level for Earth iron to flow into your bone marrow. Earth iron flow enters through the foot vortexes, communicates through the ankles, flows into the tibia and fibula, communicates through the knee into the bone marrow of the femur, communicates through the femur head, fans out through the bone marrow of the butterfly bone of the pelvis and then flows down your grounding corridor. Allow your body to make micro shifts in your seated practice while we work with running this energy, being in communication, and being grounded to your still point in the flow of mantle.

The practice is supported by letting the body make its micro shifts in the body.

Be with the soul essence sphere in the center of your head, grounded through the four aspects of grounding, the feminine, the masculine, the finite and the infinite, supported by Earth iron energy running in our bone marrow, and communicating through our red bone marrow, femur head and our butterfly bone of our pelvis.

Sky

Exhale.

Pause. In the pause of the exhale, connect thumb to pinky finger. From the center of your head and with your soul essence sphere, greet your Halo Vortex. From your soul essence in the center of your head, ask your Halo Vortex to pulse open and welcome in Sky energy.

Inhale. Allow the flow to arch back immediately to follow the inside line of the back of your skull bone.

When the flow reaches the occipital ridge it will flow down either side of the spine, underneath the long muscles of the spine, in front of the little lace muscles of the spine, and in between the large and small muscles that regulate our spine. Two channels will come down and arc through the three fused vertebrae of the sacrum. The front channel moves up the muscular structure of the abdomen on the inside line of the body through the abdominal cavity to the sternum.

As the Sky energy flow meets your shoulders, allow it to communicate through your shoulders, following your shoulders into the path of the bone at the top of the arm, (*not in the bones but following the lines of the bones*) communicating through the elbow, flowing along the two bones of the forearm, communicating through the wrist, and out the hand vortexes.

Closing of Practice

Exhale. From your soul essence in the center or aural center of the head, allow your soul essence sphere to begin contracting into the size of a grain of sand or a seed, whichever is more comfortable for you while not in active Embodied Practice.

Inhale. Inhale when you are ready.

Exhale. Soul essence contracts in. The sphere grows denser but loses no soul essence as it contracts in.

Inhale. Inhale when you are ready.

Exhale. Soul essence contracts in.

Continue your soul essence pulsation, with or without connecting thumb to pinky, as you read these words. Take as many exhales as you need until your sphere is the size of a grain of sand or a seed. Leaving it too big may create a sense of pressure or headache feeling. We also contract the soul essence sphere to a smaller size because its brilliance and energy may attract "energy vampires" who, instead of generating their own soul essence energy, would rather take ours. Contracting the sphere down to the size of a grain of sand or seed, we lose no soul essence energy, but we draw less of this unwanted attention. This protects what is precious and only ours.

Complete

Balance out any excess energy that many have built up during practice in the following way:

Relax all the muscles of the neck, allow the head to droop down, nose pointing toward the floor.

Release the arms and hands so they also droop toward the floor.

One vertebra at a time, starting from the top one nearest the neck, release the vertebra as you bend the spine slowly down, hands moving toward the floor.

Open the palms up, facing the floor for most, or for some with the flexibility the palms will touch the floor. Release any excess energy that may have built up during practice.

Imagine a pulley between your shoulder blades, and when you are ready, imagine it

pulling you up, one vertebra at a time, starting from the one closest to the tailbone.
Stack one vertebra on top of the other as the pulley moves you slowly to an upright position.

Lastly, allow your neck to rest comfortably on the atlas, the top bone of the spine.

Clearing Vortex

Note: Use this practice with the vortex clearing or daily practice clearing.

Exhale.
Pause. Coming into the pause of the exhale, bring thumb to pinky.
Inhale.
Regular breath. Allow the words about the vortex clearing to wash over you. As you work with your regular breath, make sure you stop each time in the pause of the exhale, settling in ever deeper.
Whenever there is a meeting and interchanging of two energies, the meeting creates an opening. It is much more complicated than a vortex, but we call it a clearing vortex.
Regular breath. Allow the words about the vortex clearing to wash over you. As you work with your regular breath, make sure you stop each time in the pause of the exhale, settling in ever deeper.

Exhale.
Pause. In the pause of the exhale, through your soul essence sphere, greet Earth and ask it to send a stream of energy upward, stopping 19 to 22 inches out in front of you, at nose height.
Inhale.
Exhale.
Pause. Through your soul essence sphere, greet Sky and ask Sky to drop a thin strand of energy downward to meet a strand of Earth energy.
Regular breath. The two energies will meet and will form the clearing vortex.
Exhale.
Pause. In the pause of the exhale, ask the vortex to pull into it any false information that keeps you from being embodied.
Inhale.
Exhale.
(Clear for one to two minutes.)
Pause. Ask for continued clearing. The clearing vortex will clear through all phases of the breath simply supporting you to focus in the pause of the exhale.
Inhale.
Exhale.
Pause. In the pause of the exhale, continue to clear any feelings of being out of place, allowing the vortex to support you in clearing. Take as long as you want as many breaths on each of the things we are clearing.
(Clear for one to two minutes.)
Inhale.
Exhale.

Pause. Clear any grief about losing your way through becoming disembodied. Allow yourself to sense, see, or know the clearing is occurring. Note: as we clear, our soul essence sphere brings in energy to replace the space. It is one of the soul essence functions.

(Clear for one to two minutes.)

Exhale.

Pause. In the pause of the exhale, ask Earth and Sky to retract their energy. As the energy retracts, the clearing vortex and cleared energy will dissipate.

Thank Earth and Sky for the power of their meeting.

Come out of practice as you would normally.

Settling Breath

This can be used at any time to support you in staying present or calm.

Exhale slowly.

Pause. On the pause of the exhale, connect thumb to pinky finger.

Inhale slowly.

Exhale slowly.

Pause. In the pause of the exhale, connect thumb to pinky finger. Sink, in the pause. Be with your soul essence pulse in the aural center of your head or physical center of head.

Inhale.

Release down.

Chapter 20

References

[1]Earth is estimated to be 92-94% bacteria: Referenced from Earth Times San Diego, September 1998, provided by University of Georgia, contact is William B. Whitman.

[2]Reference movement came from study of the Body in Motion DVD.

Glossary

Abyss: The space in between the photon light in the dark energy of space which, in connection, can only be held via inner mechanism.

Awakening: A beginning definition of awakening is the development of the ability to see something, where you were unable to see or understand that ability before.

Clairaudience: The ability to hear vibrational language.

Cognitive Linear Position: This is thinking that only occurs in a linear sequence, in a line – such as "1, 2, 3, …" or "A, B, C, …".

Container: This is a field or a matter container in which something else emerges from.

Electromagnetic Field of the Heart: The bio-electric field around our physical body, produced from iron in our blood flowing through our vascular system.

Flow: Always moving, but in a pulse order, or spiral relationship and connected to the pulse of the universe.

Functional Oneness: Awakening to the knowing that our position of oneness is not static. Oneness comes from our abilities to develop ourselves as energetic beings, then growing into the abilities to connect and communicate with everything.

Gathering: The collection of all photon light particles that originated from each life lived.

Human Field: This is a field which humans (over the centuries and through manipulation of energy in the ley lines of earth) brought into being over 10,000 years ago and continue to support. It is earth's distorted field, which has become the only field in which humans can develop.

Photon Light: A photon is an elementary particle, the quantum of light and all other forms of electromagnetic radiation, and the force carrier for the electromagnetic force.

Point of Origin: This is the beginning point of everything; that which begins something coming into being. Our soul essence point of origin is when the photon light from the soul pool organizes to the point of consciousness on an energy level.

Precognition: Knowledge of the future.

Reflective Relationship: This is the most beautiful to experience and most complex structure in the Universe. It is the end result of 13 billion years of evolution across the Universe. It is briefly introduced in this book. It is so complete that it cannot be defined in cognitive language.

Soul: The soul is developed each time the soul essence speaks to the chromosomes and continues to develop over each biological life.

Soul Claiming Form: The moment that the organized photon light passes in between and enters a human vortex of the sperm and egg.

Soul Essence: The photon light particles that were birthed out of or from whatever planet, solar occurrence, comet, element etc. It comes into manifest form through field relationship in the human form.

Third Eye: Refers to the abilities of the optic nerves to read photon light pictures. In Embodied Practice this is not a vortex skill, it is a skill that, if to be of use to support our evolution, must be interpreted through the second through sixth vortexes.

Visceral Intuition: Simply knowing something that cannot ultimately be put into words, because words are symbols. Visceral intuition is beyond symbols. In fact if you try and prove visceral intuition verses acting on it will become polluted.

CPSIA information can be obtained at www.ICGtesting.com
Printed in the USA
BVOW10s1838160314

347725BV00002B/3/P